SAND AND BARBED WIRE

Marjorie McCallum

MINERVA PRESS
WASHINGTON LONDON MONTREUX

SAND AND BARBED WIRE

ISBN 1 86106 343 1

First Published 1997 by
MINERVA PRESS
195 Knightsbridge
London SW7 1RE

Printed in Great Britain by
Antony Rowe Ltd, Chippenham, Wiltshire

SAND AND BARBED WIRE

Dedication

I dedicate this book to my son Ian and my daughter Susan whose young lives I hope were enriched by their experiences.

Acknowledgement

I wish to thank Susan Griffiths for her patience whilst typing this manuscript.

Foreword

Sand and Barbed Wire is the sequel to my book *Salaam Memsahib*. Both books portray the life of a wife of a regular British Army Officer serving at home and overseas.

Salaam Memsahib covers the seven and a half years my husband, Norman, served in India, *Sand and Barbed Wire* covers the three years he spent in the Canal Zone, Egypt.

Both are true accounts of how families who follow their husbands live their every day lives.

Contents

One

War Torn England

Life as the wife of a regular British Army Officer serving in India had been a great experience. I write about that period of my life in my previous book.

The period I now write about is when, after a three year separation, we are together again.

Norman, my husband, had spent seven and a half years serving in India from April 1938 to October 1945. 1 had been with him for five of those years until I was evacuated to South Africa because of wartime conditions. My baby son, Ian, was only two years old when we said farewell to Norman in Bombay.

It was 1942 and the war in Europe was at its height and the war on the Burma Front was hotting up also.

All this I recount in my recently published book *Salaam Memsahib*, my two hazardous sea voyages on Troopships, our two year stay in South Africa as evacuees and our eventual repatriation to England.

Norman's repatriation and mine did not coincide. Troopships sailing from South Africa to England were getting fewer and fewer. Many tactics were tried to get the ships safely home, ships travelling in convoy, lone ships taking a zigzag course or dashing for the home port as fast as they could, all to avoid the dangerous waters around the African coast by Lorenco Marques where the Japanese submarines lurked and sneaked out of port to torpedo our ships. In order to make sure that Ian and I arrived in England before Norman, I was advised to take a ship which landed us in England a few months before the war in Europe ended and six months before Norman's arrival.

My mother was living in Bedfordshire at this time and I was pleased to live with her until Norman came home. It had been seven years since I sailed away to India.

Mother had found it very hard that her first grandchild was four years old before she saw him. Although I longed for Norman's return, the six months we spent with my mother gave us both much happiness and also helped me to adjust to living in England again.

The war was over by the time Norman joined us in November 1945. We soon found that war-torn England posed many difficulties. When we sailed for India we had let the house we owned on the borders of Epping Forest. Now we found, because of an acute shortage of housing, we could not take possession of the house until our tenants could find alternative accommodation. Our first priority was to find a temporary home whilst we waited for the tenants to move.

My mother, who was a businesswoman and owned property in the East End of London, was away on one of her regular inspection trips when we received a phone call from her to say that she had heard of an empty flat. It was in the Epping Forest area and would we come at once to see it.

We jumped into the car (her car, as we had not yet had time to buy one of our own), and hastened to London. We picked up my mother on our way and all three of us set off to view the house. It had three storeys, two of which were let but on the ground floor was a two roomed flat with bathroom and kitchen and this was vacant. My mother, for ever with a sharp eye for property, said if we would like the flat she would buy the house and we could use the flat and when we finally got into our own house she would sell it again. There were two other couples wanting to buy and were looking over the house at the same time as us. Fortunately we knew the district well and were able to take short cuts back to the Estate Agents' Office and have the money for the deposit laid down before the other couples arrived; we beat them by minutes.

It was a few weeks before we could occupy the flat. Those weeks were not easy, harder for Norman than for me. He had come straight from a very busy life working hard on a special project for the war in Burma. He had spent the last three years in a palatial Indian house, one of the houses built by the British in the Victorian era which had been taken over by the Army and used as an Officers' Mess.

He had had no contact with children, his life being work all day and Mess life in the evenings. He had been Commanding Officer and this meant that his life was one of orderliness.

Now Norman was plunged into a household coping with wartime restrictions and the exuberance of his own small son. During the war many people were forced to work away from home. Every house owner who had a spare room was expected to accommodate one of these people. My mother had opened her house to a young man who was working on the airfield nearby. This made the house more cramped than it should have been.

I felt really sorry for Norman trying to adjust. Ian was a boisterous five year old, very happy to have his daddy around. Fortunately Ian was attending a small Dame School just along the road from my mother's house, and this gave Norman some respite from the endless games that Ian expected him to play with him.

We moved into the flat as soon as we could. We had spent the waiting time trying to piece together a home of some sort. We had not a stick of furniture and to add to our difficulties it was the time of dockets, coupons and rationing. We visited markets, attended sales and begged from our relations. China, glass, silver and kitchen utensils were no problem as we had taken all these things to India with us. These were in crates stored in the London docks. We could not house much of this stuff in a two roomed flat so there was a visit to the warehouse to take out what we wanted and leave the rest until we could move into our own house. We eventually managed to acquire sufficient furniture, carpets and curtains to furnish the flat and we moved in.

I found a very good kindergarten school for Ian just a short distance from the flat and everything seemed set for a peaceful existence.

We were waiting all the time to hear of Norman's next posting and for news from our tenants as to how they were progressing with finding alternative accommodation. News of Norman's appointment came first. He was to take command of the Holding Battalion in Bordon, Hampshire, with the acting rank of Colonel. This was surprise enough but not nearly such a shock as the knowledge that I was pregnant again. Having moved into the flat and settled Ian into school and with another baby expected there was no way we could move again.

Norman took up his appointment and was at Bordon all the week, coming home at weekends. We were happy with this arrangement, as the flat was hardly big enough for family life but was ideal for Ian and me, and we were always hoping to hear that we could take possession of the house.

The weeks slipped into months and at the end of six months we were able to move into our own house. My mother, I was very pleased to learn, had made a profit on the property she had bought to enable us to have a temporary home, when she sold it, soon after we left.

Now there really was a search for furnishings and furniture. To fill a house was much more difficult than to furnish a two roomed flat. It was surprising what things our relations found they could do without. One of my aunts gave us a three piece suite and my mother sent up her piano. The Officers' Mess in Bordon had some curtains in a cupboard, long since abandoned and these were most acceptable. It was all quite exciting.

My pregnancy was progressing well but Norman thought I needed help in the house, with his being away at Bordon during the week. Domestic help was very hard to find in post-war England. We heard that an agency was bringing over by ship young girls from Ireland who were only too eager to seek employment in England. I phoned the Agency and made enquiries. "Yes," they said, "girls were being brought over." They sent me forms which I duly filled in and returned. I was then told when a consignment of girls was expected to arrive and I was given the name of the girl they had allotted to me. The contract was binding for one year on both sides.

My father-in-law accompanied me to Euston railway station, taking me in his car to meet the boat train from Ireland. When the train drew into the station about a hundred girls poured off and were lined up on the platform. The people meeting them reported to the agent and then the search began to put together the girl and the applicant

On the paper I was carrying it said I was to meet Mary O'Leary. When asked the name of my girl I called out "Miss O'Leary". A Miss O'Leary stepped forward and the agent brought her to me. She was about seventeen years of age and looked pleasant enough if a bit dishevelled. I introduced her to my father-in-law and she asked if he was the doctor. Explaining that he was not a doctor and that he had brought me up to meet her, I put her into the back of the car and sat beside her. I tried to make her feel as happy as I could but every so often she would ask where the doctor was.

My mother-in-law had been looking after Ian for me and it was to her house we went. She had prepared an evening meal for us and we all sat down together in the dining room. We could see the girl looked uncomfortable and was not at all happy with knives and forks. The meal was fish and she got a fish bone in her mouth. Not knowing what to do with it she took it from her mouth and threw it on to the floor. My mother-in-law looked aghast at the bone landing on her very nice dining room carpet.

We were to spend the night at the house of my in-laws, going home to our house in the morning. A kind neighbour was going to put Miss O'Leary up for the night and I suggested that all she took with her were her night clothes and her tooth brush and I would look after her luggage. She said she did not have night clothes and then burst into tears saying, “Where is the doctor?” At this stage, being completely at a loss to know what to do I asked to see her papers. There I found she had been allotted to a doctor in North London and that her name was Helen O’Leary. I looked again at my papers and found that I had Mary O’Leary written on mine. I had obviously brought home the wrong girl. My mistake had been calling out only the surname and not the Christian name before it.

I tried to pacify the poor girl as well as I could promising I would take her back to London in the morning. I phoned the doctor in North London. He had not retrieved my girl and I wondered if I would find her. I began to wish that I had not embarked on this scheme at all. The next morning saw us back at the Agents where Mary was waiting to be collected. To my great relief Mary seemed a much nicer girl. She was older, round and plump and from all appearances not as raw as Helen O’Leary who I handed back to the Agent.

It was a shock when Mary told me that when the ship docked at Liverpool the girls were taken ashore and plunged into baths and forcibly made to wash their hair. It really was like sorting out cattle, and Mary was most indignant.

Mary stayed with us for over the year. On the whole she was pleasant enough but annoyed me greatly when on Sundays she refused to do any work at all saying she was Roman Catholic and her religion would not allow her to work on Sundays. She would not even flick a duster over the house and yet she wanted also her day off a week. She must have come from a large family for every so often, after receiving letters from Ireland I would find her in floods of tears, she would throw herself into a chair wailing and rocking to and fro saying her second cousin or one of her Uncles had died. Nothing would pacify her and gloom would prevail over the kitchen for days. The only way I could pull her out of her moods was to suggest that she caught the next boat home. This worked wonders as the prospect of returning home to no work made her realise she was better off here in England.

It was getting near the end of my pregnancy and we were both getting anxious, with Norman away all the week only coming home at weekends, that nothing should go wrong with the arrangements I had made for the birth of the baby. I had booked for my confinement a room in a local maternity home with my own doctor in attendance. I had about three weeks to go before the baby was expected.

I had promised Norman that I would visit the maternity home to see if they had my room safely booked and that all was in order. I went on the Thursday and was greeted at the door by the Matron with the words, "Please don't be early as we are shut for two weeks." When I asked her why, I was told that they had had an enteric epidemic and that one baby had died and the home was closed whilst fumigation was taking place.

When Norman came home on Friday I greeted him with this news. His reaction was quite upsetting. He began to pace the room, as was his wont when in distress. He said, "How can I go back to Bordon and leave things like this? What will happen if you are early?" The next morning he phoned the doctor and told him some arrangement had to be made before he left on Monday morning. From the tone of his voice I am sure the doctor was left in no doubt that he had to do something. On Sunday evening we heard that a private room had been booked at Queen Mary Hospital at Stratford in the East End of London and I was to be a private patient of the resident obstetrician. Norman left for Bordon on Monday a happier man.

I was to visit the hospital during the coming week to have checks and to meet the doctor. The following week I went again for a visit but this time I was kept in. That evening Norman received a message to say that he had a lovely baby daughter and that mother and baby were doing well. I was very comfortable in the hospital. I had a large room and was able to have my baby in a cot beside my bed.

During the next afternoon Norman arrived at the hospital. He was wearing his uniform having been driven from Bordon in a staff car. He caused quite a stir wearing the red tabs of his recent promotion to acting Colonel. He looked so young to be holding such a high rank, and indeed he was, being only thirty-five.

His arms were full of flowers and there was a huge smile on his face which grew even larger when the nurse told him his daughter looked like him. Apparently there had been a riotous evening in the Mess when the news leaked out.

We had decided that if the baby was a girl we would call her Susan. I had spoken to Ian, who was now six years old, on the phone, to tell him about his baby sister. He said, “Mummy, is she tiny and when can I see her?” When I told him she was tiny and had black hair, he said, “I haven’t got black hair so why has the baby got black hair?” I told him that she looked just like Daddy and Daddy had black hair. He accepted that and I heard him call to my mother, who was looking after him in the house, “Granny, my baby sister has got black hair.”

It was quite an experience being a private patient in such a hospital. The nurses would whisper outside my door and one evening a nurse was just coming through the door with a mug of cocoa in her hand, when one of the other nurses shouted to her, “Don’t take that in there like that, she’s private and must have a saucer.” That really made me laugh.

Norman stayed at home with Ian for the rest of the week, with Mary O’Leary looking after them. He said that he would take Ian back to Bordon with him the next week. Bordon was holding two hundred WRACs waiting to be posted, so there was no lack of helping hands for Norman looking after Ian. Two WRACs, when off duty, took Ian into town on a shopping expedition. They went into a butcher’s shop taking Ian in with them. Ian, looking around, saw a leg of lamb lying on the counter. Pointing to it, he said “Does the lamb know his leg is lying there?” On another occasion when they had been out with Ian and were coming back into the camp Ian saw a senior

Officer with only one arm. Ian, in a loud voice exclaimed, "What's he done with his other arm?" No wonder Norman was back home before the week was out.

It was wonderful to take my lovely baby daughter home on the Sunday. The house was full of relations and friends eager to see the baby. My father-in-law had managed to acquire two bottles of champagne and he soon had glasses charged and led the toast for the baby's future. Ian was jumping up and down with excitement and I had to be so careful that he did not squeeze Susan too hard when he held her.

We soon settled down into a routine and the days were very busy indeed. I had learnt to cope with making meals from the meagre rations we were allowed whilst I was in the flat. I became adept at cooking cakes without fat and using dried eggs. I never ceased to admire the British housewives for their ability to produce good nourishing meals from the small amounts of meat, cheese and fats that were the weekly ration.

Whale meat was introduced and if you were lucky you could get the occasional rabbit. Should you know somebody who kept chickens then there might be an egg for one of the children. A special ration of orange juice, rose-hip syrup and cod liver oil was allocated for the children. We had a plum tree in the garden and I remember Ian complaining bitterly that we either had plums and custard or custard and plums for pudding every day.

My father-in-law had a ship repairing works in the London docks. One day a ship came in with a cargo of coconut oil. The oil had spilled over and blocked some of the pumps. His firm was called in to free them. The oil was white and thick and instead of wasting it he put it into tins and brought it home. The family, friends and neighbours lived on beautiful coconut cakes for weeks; after fat-less cakes it was much appreciated. He also brought us tins of cocoa, powdered milk and sugar already mixed and by just adding hot water this made an excellent bedtime drink – a rare treat!

"Make do and mend," was the slogan of the day. Overcoats, if they were shabby, would be un-picked, turned and sewn up afresh. Evening dresses were cut up to make party dresses for children. Bed sheets, when worn thin in the middle, would be cut and sewn sides to middle with a nice flat seam, or made into pillow cases. Parachute silk, collected from used parachutes, made excellent underwear. Nothing was wasted and the ingenuity of the housewife was amazing and I am sure satisfaction was the just reward.

Susan was a happy, contented baby and growing fast. We had had a good long stretch of time without a new posting for Norman, but it was inevitable that it would come. The posting was going to help us this time as Norman was to become a substantive colonel and command the REME Headquarters' workshops in Ashford, Middlesex. He would be able to live at home if he travelled the thirty-five miles night and morning by car. It was a tiring journey but it was lovely to have him live at home with us. I had many duties to perform as the wife of the Commanding Officer; I was expected to attend most of the social functions, organise children's parties and present prizes at sports days.

I remember once at a sports day there was a tug-of-war, and it was between the men from Wimpey and the local Army team. The Wimpey team won and the men were lined up for me to shake hands with them. The firm of Wimpey employed men of great stature and strength which their work of heavy engineering and road making demanded. They were enormous with huge hands and when they shook my hand I could have cried out at each grasp and was thankful to have a hand without broken fingers at the end of the line.

Ian was attending a small private school a short distance along the road. Mary or I would take and fetch him until he was old enough to walk along by himself.

It was the winter of 1947, a cruel harsh winter with many weeks of snow and ice in January and February. The snow lay thick everywhere and as fast as the roads were cleared it snowed again. It would thaw slightly and then freeze again leaving great ruts of hard compacted snow on the roads and pavements. In our area the river Lea burst its banks and the water contaminated the local reservoir. In consequence the water was cut off, we did not even have stand pipes. Water carts would come round once a day ringing a bell to alert householders to come with their buckets to fetch their water. Every drop of water was used with care and with two children, one still only a baby, it was quite a hardship. Mary O'Leary was not at all cooperative in saving water. Hot water bottles to put in our beds to keep us warm at night were essential. The water for these had to be used over and over again, re-heating the water every night. Twice Mary emptied the water out of her bottle and this made me very cross as the precious water that I was saving for the children had to be used.

One day when I was upstairs feeding the baby I heard the water cart arriving outside ringing its bell. I called to Mary to collect the buckets and take them outside to be filled. She refused, saying she had a headache. Hurriedly I put Susan into her cot and leaving her screaming because her feed had been interrupted, rushed downstairs, picked up the buckets and ran after the cart which by this time was a good many yards up the road.

The next day Norman was relating this story in the Officers' Mess when the Mess Sergeant heard him. "I have an idea, sir," he said and went out of the room. That evening when Norman went to his car to start his journey home, he found a smiling Mess Sergeant standing by his car with a small beer barrel at his feet. He had washed the barrel well and now it was full of clean drinking water. The Sergeant said that the water might taste a little beery but at least it was good drinking water. What a blessing this water was. Norman would take the barrel back every morning and bring it home full in the evening, tasting less beery as the days went by. I wrote to the sergeant to thank him for his quick thinking when he heard the story. It was indeed a kind act.

We were thankful when winter slipped into spring and summer. Mary gave in her notice at the beginning of the summer. She had been with us over the year but now wanted to take up employment nearer to friends she had made on the other side of London. I was not sorry but knew that without Mary in the house I would find things difficult domestically. We thought we would plan a holiday and on our return I could then think about a replacement for Mary.

It was a great problem to know where to go with two children. Not many people were taking holidays as they were still feeling the effects of the war. Many of our beaches had been mined and were not free from danger.

One evening when we were puzzling our brains as to where we should go Norman remembered Norfolk. The story of Norman's connection with Norfolk went back many years. Friends of his parents owned a large house on the edge of the largest of the Norfolk Broads, Hickling. The owner of the house, Mr Humby, had had the house built to his own specification at the turn of the twentieth century. It was to be a retreat from his busy life in London where he had a thriving dental practice. He was a lover of the outdoor life, also a lover of people and he had a very generous nature. He liked nothing better than to invite his friends to the house to enjoy the many delights this corner of England held – and they were many.

The Broads provided water sports in every form. Sailing with half-deckers and sailing dinghies; rowing boats and quanting punts. Hours could be spent birdwatching with the reward of seeing a cormorant or a heron amongst the ducks and the coots. Fishing enthusiasts would go out in rowing boats in the early morning, content to fish all day, coming home in the evening with their catch. The Broad held pike, bream, roach, perch and trench and the occasional eel could be caught if one escaped the net of the old eel-catcher. The eel-catcher was a charming old man. He would have his nets which were round in a long tube with hoops of wire every so often to keep the tube open, stretched across a narrow part of the dyke and lying as deep as possible. A red flag flew so you knew when he was there.

It was alright if the sailing boats were not having to tack up the stream. When a boat was tacking he would stand up on the bank, doff his cap and say in a broad Norfolk accent, "There be nets down there, watch your wake." He was a real character.

For the guns, hide-outs carefully made amongst the reeds were vantage points for shooting wild fowl, ducks and coots. In the close-season a clay pigeon trap was erected in the paddock beside the house.

Organised coot shoots were arranged with one local man quanting a punt or light rowing boat, with one of the party with a gun in each boat forming a half circle before the shooting began. Large Wherry boats were used for dredging the broads, and on regatta days the Wherries were commissioned for the Committee and the Judges. The sea was only three miles away where the lovely golden sands were thought to be crowded if more than ten people were on the beach at one time. If one tired of all this then there was always tennis or croquet on the well-kept lawn in front of the house.

It was here, in this idyllic place, where Norman in his youth had learned to sail, fish and shoot when he joined his parents at the house parties that Mr Humby organised. Mr Humby in his hey-day knew that if the Guest House, aptly named, was to be always ready for when he, his family and friends, wanted to visit, then he must have a resident staff to run it. He looked around, and at the local Inn he found 'just what he was looking for'. The Inn Keeper who had a large family, comprising his wife, four daughters and seven sons, was complaining one day that now that his family was growing up the accommodation at the Inn was too cramped and that he needed to seek employment with better housing for his family.

Mr Humby could see what an advantage it would be to have this hard working family working for him at the Guest House, and how it would lessen the anxieties for the Inn Keeper.

By 1910, four of the sons had gone to America to make new lives for themselves and one son had married and lived in the village. This left four daughters and two sons to be moved into the house. At first the mother and father did most of the work with the children as they grew older taking on responsibilities.

Norfolk folk are kind gentle people, content and hardworking and this family by the name of Beales stayed and looked after the Humby family for many years.

My introduction to Hickling and the Guest House came in later years when I went with Norman for two summers before we were married, and I liked it so much that I agreed to spend one week of our honeymoon there.

By this time Mr Humby was a very elderly gentleman and could not travel to Norfolk anymore. The house was being run just as it always had been with the Beales family in charge. Norman would take me to see Mr and Mrs Humby in their London home and it gave them much joy to hear we had spent time in their beloved house in Norfolk.

Whilst we were overseas we heard that the old gentleman had died. In his will he bequeathed the Guest House to his granddaughter with the proviso that the Beales family, who had served him so faithfully, should be allowed to remain in the house. It was Mr Humby's intention that the Beales family should be able to make a profitable living for themselves by continuing the flow of visitors to the Guest House. It was not too long before they had built up a business of repute based on the regular visitors and recommendation.

All this we remembered when we were pondering our holiday arrangements. We wrote off and when the reply came they said that they would be delighted to have us for two weeks. Very happy at the news we packed and off we went.

When we arrived it was like stepping back in time, we could hardly believe our eyes, even the furniture in the rooms was the same and everything was spic and span just like it always had been.

Two of the daughters had married and gone away. This left three of the Beales family in residence, Mabel, Ruby and the middle son Percy, with Waldo the younger son, now married and living with his wife Iris in a bungalow on the edge of the dyke overlooking the boathouses, popping in occasionally to give a hand.

Mabel and Ruby had not changed in the eleven years that we had been away. Mabel still had her wonderful sense of humour and Waldo also, there was always much laughter in the house. Mabel was a superb cook; I can taste the wonderful fruit pies she cooked to this day and her roast beef and Yorkshire pudding, with vegetables grown by Percy in the garden, has never been surpassed. There had always been three reception rooms in the house and when the house was full it could take three families at one time, each family using one of the rooms as a private sitting room where all meals were served to them.

Ruby had always served meals in this way. It was very hard work for her, so sometimes a young girl from the village would come to help her.

For the visitors this was a unique arrangement and Ruby, in spite of the hard work, with her placid and conscientious nature had never thought of altering the arrangements to lighten her work.

Percy looked after the garden, the outside and inside maintenance and kept the tennis court in order. Work for him in the house was made a little lighter now that electricity had been brought to the village as he no longer had to fill and trim the oil lamps and put them in the rooms. Water, however, had not yet been piped to the village so he still had the task of pumping all the water for the house from the old fashioned water pump outside the kitchen door. Morning and night he would light the copper in the outside wash-house to heat the water to be carried upstairs to the bedrooms for the use of the guests. If a bath was needed it was a major operation and had to be ordered some hours before. On top of all this there were the outside lavatories with the buckets which had to be emptied and the wooden seat to be kept fresh.

Percy plodded through the work, the only time we ever saw him sitting down was when he was sitting under the apple tree in the orchard, shelling peas.

As soon as we could, after settling ourselves in, we went to visit Waldo and Iris in their bungalow, and then to look at the Boat Houses. Waldo had looked after the boats from the very early days. Now he had built a third boathouse on to the existing two. It was a joy to go into them. They had corrugated iron roofs and the sides were made from reeds; they were built on the edge of the dyke with the water flowing through them. Everything was immaculate with the sailing boats with their sails beautifully furled and their ropes neatly coiled. Waldo had also enlarged the garage which was next to his bungalow. Since the coming of the electricity to the village his one petrol pump now boasted an electric motor, before this event we used to watch him pump the petrol up by working a hand lever from side to side; when he first started the garage he only sold petrol in green tins.

In 1919 he bought his first car, a second-hand Studebaker with a collapsible pram-like hood.

In the early days visitors to the Guest House would travel from London to Wroxham by train, then on by a smaller train to a halt called Catfield, here a horse and trap would be waiting for them with Mr Beales Senior driving. When Waldo got his Studebaker he would motor in to Wroxham to fetch the guests.

Our holiday was a most happy one, the children thrived on the lovely Norfolk air and good food, rationing was not much in evidence with the produce from Percy's garden and with the chickens and ducks running about. Ian was in seventh heaven in the boat houses and loved to help Waldo put away the boats at dusk.

Two

Posted To Egypt

On returning from holiday I had two priorities; the first to find a replacement for Mary, the second to find a good preparatory school for Ian. I set about the domestic help first by placing an advertisement in the local newspaper.

I knew the type of person I wanted and that was somebody to come in for two days a week to look after the children. I did not mind hard work just as long as I could get out occasionally. From the answers to my advertisement I found just the right person. She was middle-aged and had a grown-up family of her own. Her name was Mrs Wilcher and she loved children. She had a sunny nature and was always singing. Invariably I knew when she was arriving; she would come in by the back garden gate singing, "Oh! What a beautiful morning; Oh what a beautiful day."

If I had been out in the morning I would sometimes return around teatime. Then I would find her and the children blissfully happy sitting around the kitchen stove making toast or toasting crumpets. I deemed myself very fortunate in finding such a treasure and the children loved her.

The only problem I had was a lack of transport, with Norman using the only car we had. I must, unknowingly, have conveyed this problem to Norman for one day he said that he had a surprise for me. I was to go upstairs and promise not to look over the banisters and he would call me when he was ready. I did as I was asked, firmly shutting the bedroom door.

I heard a lot of opening and shutting of doors and bumping going on and the children in high spirits helping with whatever was going on.

When I was allowed to come downstairs and into the hall, which was a large square hall, I had the surprise of my life. There before my eyes was a most beautiful ladies' motorcycle. It was a 'James Comet' – a proper two stroke motorbike. "Now," Norman said, "you will be able to get about."

I was blissfully happy with my motorbike and on the days when Mrs Wilcher came I went all over the place. I had a dear Aunt who lived only ten miles away and I would visit her, which gave me much pleasure. She lived alone but always managed to give me a nice tea and I often wondered how she did it on the meagre rations allowed for one person, but then I would always take her something that I could spare from home. When Susan started at the local kindergarten school I had a child seat fixed to the pillion of the bike and would take her to school strapped into the seat. She loved it. Traffic on the roads in the 1940s and '50s was, compared with traffic of today in the 1990s, very light, and motoring was a pleasure.

Ian had a pedal bike and on nice sunny days we all three would cycle to the swimming pool, Susan and I on the motor bike and Ian coming along behind on his bicycle. I was more than delighted with these arrangements.

Having transport helped me to visit preparatory schools in the area. I would do the preliminary inspections of the schools and Norman would follow with a more serious viewing of the schools I favoured. We chose one in the Woodford area and Ian was to start as a day boy in September.

We went on happily like this until one day Norman arrived home with his face wearing his worried look. I always knew when something was worrying him as he would stand and look at me making quite sure that he had my full attention before saying what he had to say. I had guessed what it would be – yes, another posting.

I found it very hard to listen to what he had to say – I just wanted to blot it all out. The posting was to Egypt, the Suez Canal Zone. If I had not been so wrapped up in my own happiness and had read the daily newspapers more, I would have read about the troubles in the Suez Canal Zone and how the British Armed Forces were stationed there in large numbers protecting our interests whilst unrest was raging all around them. The British armed forces were guarding imperial lines of communication through Egypt, between the Mediterranean Sea and the Red Sea, particularly in the Suez Canal Zone. The Anglo-Egyptian Treaty of Friendship and Alliance made in 1936 was abrogated by the then Egyptian Government, the Wafd, and in 1951 hostilities broke out against the British. The British were standing firm and enlarged the military presence in the Zone.

Norman's new appointment was to the General Staff of the Directorate of Electrical and Mechanical Engineers, at the General Headquarters of the Middle East Land Forces, which were stationed at Fayid on the edge of the Great Bitter Lake. He was to report to a troopship sailing from Liverpool in three weeks' time. He was told that his family could follow him in a few weeks, providing the situation did not deteriorate.

I was devastated by all this news. We had had a long stretch without a posting, enjoying family life so much and now we were faced with upheaval and separation again. There was no time to indulge in miseries; there was so much to be done.

Although I had learnt that the Canal Zone was a Families Station I knew I could not take Ian to Egypt with me. He was just eleven years old and his education was of paramount importance. Susan was just five and she could continue her education at the schools provided by the Army in the Canal Zone.

The awful thought of leaving Ian at home in boarding school haunted me day and night. He would have his grandparents near by which gave me a little comfort.

Only too soon I was saying farewell to Norman at Euston railway station on his way to join the troopship in Liverpool. I was deep in thought as I drove home trying to think how I was to cope with all I had to do and found it difficult to know where to start.

We had decided to let our house, on the borders of Epping Forest, furnished to the Army. This would give us the security of being able to repossess on our return. Norman's posting was for three years.

I first went to see the Headmaster of Ian's school and arranged for him to become a boarder when the term started in September. I knew it would take me until then to make my preparations to leave. To let the house furnished was my next job. I contacted the Housing Authorities of the Army and they sent along a Major, his wife and their one son of about Ian's age, to view the house. It was a Saturday and Ian was at home. Had I known how badly the fact that another family was coming to live in our house would upset him, I would have arranged another day for the viewing. The couple's young son seemed to delight in showing off and when they got to Ian's bedroom he declared that that was his bedroom and proceeded to pick up Ian's precious belongings as if they were his own. I shall never forget the pain on Ian's face and when the boy saw Ian's goldfish bowl and said he would have that, Ian's emotions overflowed into real tears. I quickly said that the goldfish and bowl were going with Ian and that his grandparents were going to look after them. This saved the day, but it made me realise how badly Ian was taking the breaking up of our home.

I applied to the Embarkation Authorities and asked for a passage as soon as possible after the second week in September when Ian would have started the new term at school as a boarder.

I now devoured the daily newspapers for every bit of news on the situation in the Canal Zone. It would fluctuate between hostilities and calm and nobody knew where they were at all. I forged ahead with the packing and making arrangements to have the car put up on blocks and stored in the garage. Norman said I should coat all the works of the motorbike with preservative before I put that into the garage for storage.

The house was let at the beginning of August and I took two rooms in a private hotel which had recently opened almost opposite the house.

I left my half-packed baggage in the hotel and took the two children off to Norfolk to the Guest House for two weeks holiday. I wanted to spend as much time as possible with Ian before leaving him in school. I borrowed my mother's car for the holiday which was a great blessing for me. When we arrived at the Guest House we received a very warm welcome from the Beales family, and Norfolk seemed so peaceful after the hustle and bustle of the past weeks.

I hired a sailing dinghy for the two weeks and we were out in the boat most days, with Ian learning to sail the boat very quickly. Our favourite occupation was to sail right across the Broad to a small island called 'Ma Turner's Island'. Here we would tie up, go ashore to have our picnic and explore the island. Ian and Susan loved to climb the trees – a good vantage point for watching the birds and looking at the other craft on the water. The weather was not being kind to us; although we had the wind for sailing, we had rain and cold as well. The East Coast can be very treacherous in these conditions. Whenever we went to the beach it was a case of having to shelter from the cold winds amongst the sand dunes. We would come in in the early evening from sailing or the beach, wet and cold and thankful to spend a cosy evening in our own private sitting-room at the Guest House, playing games and partaking of an excellent meal prepared by Mabel.

Ian's enjoyment in the art of sailing was rewarding for me as I was finding all this activity very exhausting. The strain of packing up our home and looking after the children single-handed, plus the cold wet weather, took its toll on me. I went down with a severe chill; fortunately it came at the end of the holiday.

On the way home I called in at my mother's house to ask her if I could keep the car until my passage came through. She took one look at me, put me to bed and sent for the doctor. He diagnosed pneumonia. My mother was in the throes of moving house from Bedfordshire to Essex and it was most inconvenient for her to have a sick daughter with two children descend upon her. I was forced to rest up for a few days but then began to worry about my unpacked baggage and Ian's school trunk. I went back to the hotel calling in to my doctor on the way. She was a personal friend of mine as well as being my doctor. She told me that I had to rest and if I didn't she said I would not be fit to take up my passage to Egypt when it came. What a plight I was in!

It was the children I was worried about. I had a dear friend whose daughter was in the same class as Susan at school. She took Susan off my hands every day returning her to me at bedtime. Ian spent most days at the doctor's house, she having a son and daughter around his age.

It was a warm September and I sat in the garden of the hotel for many hours basking in the warm sunshine. I gradually regained sufficient strength to finish the packing and to spend more time with Ian.

I had been told by the Colonel in charge of families that they were planning to fly the school children out to the Canal Zone for the Christmas and summer holidays. This helped Ian and me very much as we were able to count the weeks until the Christmas holidays when he would be able to join us.

I had not heard from the Embarkation Authorities and so I began to agitate, phoning at least once a week. I was receiving letters from Norman telling me of the difficulties the men were experiencing getting their families out to join them. It appeared that there was a points system operating whereby points were given on length of service, availability of quarters and length of separation. I hoped by the time my passage came through Norman would have sufficient points to enable me to join him.

The weeks slipped by, the summer holidays were over and the school term was starting. I dreaded the day coming when I would have to put Ian into boarding school and say farewell to him. It was the hardest task I have ever undertaken and to this day I cannot think how I ever managed to get through it.

I took Ian to the school one evening after lessons were over. The Headmaster was very kind and understanding. He left us alone in his study for a while, but this made things worse as we were both too upset to talk. I had left Susan at her grandparents' house. When I went to fetch her, I stopped the car outside the house but it was a good twenty minutes before I could go in. I walked up and down the road to try to compose myself. I did not want Susan to see me in distress.

My heart goes out to all parents who, because of their way of life in the Services, Diplomatic Corps, Civil Service or Commerce, have to leave their children in boarding school to be educated whilst they are serving overseas. Now that Ian has children of his own, he often says to me, "You had to do it, Mother."

It is a very foolish wife who does not follow her husband. There is always someone out there who will comfort your husband when he is down; I have seen it happen too many times.

Within a week, I received notification from the War Office that I was booked on the troopship *The Empress of Australia*, sailing from Liverpool on October 25th. I was sent a Warrant for my heavy baggage with a date for its collection. Imagine my consternation when two days later I received another message telling me that our sailing date was being put forward by twenty days and that we were to embark on another troopship, *The Empire Test*, on October 5th. Panic stations! – How was I going to be ready? Many things did not get done such as farewells to relatives and friends, but we made it. I was ready in time for my father-in-law to take Susan and me to Euston station to catch our train to Liverpool.

I had taken books, pencils and card games to amuse Susan on the long train journey. On arriving at the docks we saw *Empire Test* alongside. The ship looked so small it did not seem possible that she could be a troopship. I learned afterwards that *The Empire Test* was the smallest ship in the fleet.

The passengers, all service wives and children with as many troops on the lower decks as the ship could hold, were either on deck or filing up the gangplanks to board. The women were far too tired to be sociable and just went about their business of finding their cabins and settling themselves in with a kind of resignation that verged on despair.

Susan and I were shown, by one of the ship's stewards, to a cabin on the sun deck in a most favourable position in the ship. It was a four berth cabin and most spacious. Everybody was very quiet going down to dinner and retiring early for the night. The scene the following morning as we went down to breakfast was quite different; the women smiled and made conversation and the crew were pleasant and helpful.

During the morning a steward came to me saying that the Captain sent his compliments and would like me to join him for coffee in his cabin at eleven o'clock. This puzzled me a bit but I dutifully went along taking Susan with me. The Captain and the First Engineer greeted us; they were both charming and welcomed us aboard. The steward came in with coffee and a glass of orange squash for Susan. I soon found the reason for such an early invitation. It appeared that I was the only Colonel's wife on board and as such was Senior Lady. I then learned that I was expected to take charge of the social side of life for the Army wives and children. The Captain asked me if I would organise a school for the children; two hours in the morning and one and a half hours in the afternoon. He explained that because the ship was so small it was necessary to organise the children to keep them out of the way of the crew when they were at work. They said they would give me every assistance possible and told me that there was some school equipment available. I was rather taken aback by this request – I was only just recovering from the bout of pneumonia and did not feel at all strong. However, there is nothing like a purpose to get one going and I knew I must do the best I could.

That afternoon an announcement was pinned to the notice board saying a meeting of all wives was to be held in the lounge that evening. There was a good turn out; I presided and the Captain attended. I asked for suggestions and volunteers, searching as I did so for any talents amongst the women. Two of them had had teacher training so that was going to be a great help. I drew up a rota system and pinned it to the noticeboard and we started the school the next morning. It really was good, as even if we had started the journey with lethargy, everybody snapped out of it quickly and the mothers were soon laughing and planning, with the children eager to get started. Sometimes there would be a knock on my cabin door with a message to say a 'Mrs so & so' had not reported for duty and they needed help, but that did not happen very often.

Every evening I was expected to attend a small cocktail party in the Captain's cabin. He would only ask a few of the wives at a time and he relied on me to help entertain them. I had to bath Susan and have her in her bunk by six o'clock. She was such a good girl and never once complained, sensing I think that Mummy had a job to do. She felt quite safe as the Captain's steward kept an eye on her and I was, in any case, only two cabins away from her.

After the school had been running for a few days, the Captain asked me if there was anything I needed. "Yes," I said, "I need all the pencils and crayons sharpened." "That is no problem," he said and asked me to bring all the pencils to his cabin after school, which would be teatime. There, the First Engineer and the Captain got busy with their penknives. The First Engineer had been busy trying to sew a button on his tunic. He was making such a mess of it that I offered to sew it on for him and did so. It was quite a domestic scene with the two men sharpening pencils and me sewing on the button.

I was feeling stronger day by day and enjoying the atmosphere of the ship, which was like one happy family. The crew were so friendly and helpful but they did tease us a lot. They would receive news over the ship's wireless and relay to us the happenings in the Canal Zone. The relationship between the Egyptian Government and the British seemed to be deteriorating. When the news was bad the crew would tease us saying, "You won't see your husbands this trip, we will be taking you home again." We would laugh, thinking it was only teasing, and would dismiss it as just fun. Little did we know how real it was. The morning came when we anchored off Port Said soon after sunrise. Everything was very still. The women were all on deck searching the horizon for signs of their husbands. The hours ticked by; the crew were not teasing us now but went about their business with concern.

Susan and I went down for a quick breakfast, then hurried up on deck again. There was a stillness about the place; no clatter of a busy dock; all was quiet and eerie. We seemed to be looking out for some sign of life for hours and began to wonder if we would be allowed ashore at all. Presently we spotted a boat leaving the shore and heading towards the ship. We could see that there were about ten men in the boat all clad in military uniforms. I borrowed somebody's binoculars and saw one of the men was Norman. He quickly reached us on deck and said we must hurry off the ship as quickly as we could. Picking up our baggage we boarded the small boat and were whisked away very speedily to the shore. I had no time to say farewell to the other wives and could not see any of them as we were being propelled in haste to the shore. Fond greetings went by the board and in their place were stealth and urgency. When we reached the shore Norman said we were to sit in the car, which was parked on the side of the dock, whilst he went into a wooden building to change out of his uniform into civilian clothes. I had no time to tell him how much I liked the very smart new Fiat car he had bought. He had driven from Fayid to Ismailia and then on to Port Said to meet us. Now we were to do the journey in reverse and from what he said it was likely to be hazardous.

We were told that should we be stopped we were to leave all the talking to Norman; Susan and I were not to say a word. We were to pretend to be Canal Company Staff and it was hoped we would get away with it, with Norman's uniform well hidden as a precaution. Susan caught the tension in the atmosphere from us and sat in the back of the car as quiet as a mouse.

We reached Ismailia safely and went into the United Services' Club for lunch. Here we could relax and greet one another properly. It had been an interesting drive alongside the Canal. It was sand and sand dunes for miles and miles with small oases of date palms and native huts with goats and donkeys dotted about. The ships going through the canal seemed to slide along rather than float. Sometimes the dunes would be so high that only the funnels or masts of the ships could be seen as they passed through the cutting of the Canal.

The Sweet Water Canal ran alongside the road. This is reputed to be the most polluted water possible. It is said that if someone fell in the water, he would be likely to end up with all sorts of terrible diseases – so everyone kept well away from the Sweet Water Canal.

In the Ismailia Club, Susan spotted a cat; it was the most mangy cat I had ever seen. Susan loved cats and she adored the one we had at home which was a lovely ginger one. She ran to pick up this cat – just in time I shouted to her not to touch it. She could not understand that she could not fondle it and it took a lot of explaining as to why she was not allowed to do so.

We then sped on our journey. Reaching Fayid was quite an experience. Norman pointed out places of interest: the General Headquarters, depots and barracks, all surrounded by barbed wire, with armed sentries at the gates and around the perimeters. We were heading for Kensington Village which was to be our home for the next two and a half years. Kensington Village was where the Officers and their families lived and it was the size of a small village in England. It housed the quarters, the Army School, the Anglican Church, sports grounds, tennis courts and clinics. It was completely surrounded by barbed wire with a road block at the entrance with armed guards and armed patrols on the perimeter. Other facilities, such as the 'NAAFI', where we did all our shopping, and the small native shops, where there was always a camel and its owner waiting to give rides to the children, (the camel's name was 'Telephone', and he earned a lot of money for his owner) were outside the barbed wire. The NAAFI, an acronym for 'The Navy, Army and Air Force Institute', was the main supplier of all we needed.

The Officers' Club and that of the Non-Commissioned Officers, together with the Troops' Beach, were located on the shore of the Great Bitter Lake.

Susan looked very frightened when we were stopped by the armed guards as we went through the roadblock at the entrance to Kensington Village; she hated the guns they held. She never really lost her fear of them for the whole two and a half years we were there. No matter how much we told her that the soldiers were there for our protection and that they were her friends, she still was not convinced. When ever we walked through the gate she would take a large circle around them keeping as much distance as possible between herself and them.

We were to spend one week as guests of our Major General and his wife in their quarter on 'Red Flannel Alley', the name that was given to the row of quarters that held the senior Officers of the rank of Colonel and above who wore red flannel tabs on their jacket lapels and around their caps, denoting their senior rank.

Although it was most kind of the Major General and his wife to entertain us, I found it a strain not having met them before. It was restricting for Susan, and I found living in the General's house had its limitations for me in the meeting of other wives.

Our quarter was ready at the end of the week and we moved in. The quarters were all alike and were single storey, oblong in shape, having four large square rooms side by side. They were brick built with corrugated iron roofs which came down over two verandas running the whole length of the house both front and back.

Each room had four windows, two front and two back and three doors. Two of these doors, one front and one back, led out on to the veranda while the third door led into the next room. An electric fan hung from the ceiling in each room and one wall was taken up entirely by large built-in cupboards. The bathroom, lavatory, kitchen and pantry were in a separate building connected to the quarter by a covered way.

The lavatory was primitive in the extreme. It was a cubicle within the outer building and comprised a high wooden seat with a hole in the middle under which was a large bucket. In the outside wall was a wooden flap and once a day a cart with two servants would tour the compounds to empty the buckets. The flap would be raised and the bucket whisked away - this could be rather embarrassing if one was in situ at the time!

There was one other building in the compound; this was also a square room and was for the use of your servant. Although the quarters were basic, they were adequate. It was surprising how different each one looked from the other when the occupants put their own individualities into them.

At the front of each quarter was a cultivated garden and at the back a large expanse of sand which had to be swept every day by your servant. He used a large piece of sacking tied on to a broom handle. This he pulled over the sand to make it smooth. It looked very untidy if it was not swept.

The compound was fenced in by a low wire mesh, with a wooden gate at the front entrance. The cars were kept beside the quarters in a car-port which consisted of a framework surrounded by sacking. This kept the sun off the car and some of the wind blown sand.

The irrigation system for the gardens was ingenious. Each quarter had a pipe system in a gully running the whole length of the garden. At each end of the gully was a bung. Set days and times were laid down for the irrigation of one's garden. On the appropriate day and time either you or your servant would go out to operate the two bungs. The bung on the side from which the water was to flow into your gully would be taken out and the water would come in. The bung at the other end of the garden would be firmly put in place to stop the water flowing out. A time was set, after which the bung on your neighbours' side would be taken out to allow him to water his garden.

This system caused much trouble and ill feeling, as enthusiastic gardeners would use it out of turn. There was one Officer who tried to grow pineapples in his garden. He was seen going out after dark to utilise the system out of turn, for the sake of his pineapples. I spent two days unpacking and making the quarter look like home.

The next day I took Susan along to the Army School. This was a building similar to the quarters in construction but larger in order to accommodate the children. The Headmistress, who had recently arrived in the Zone from Scotland, was a most pleasant person. Susan seemed immediately at ease in her company and enjoyed the tour of the school. The classrooms were light and colourful with all the projects the children had made pinned around the walls. The school was not overcrowded and the children looked happy.

Susan was to start lessons the next morning. We would have to be up early in the morning as the children started school early and finished at lunch time. These times fitted in better with the climate, especially in the hot weather. The next morning I watched as Susan ran up the road bracing herself against a wind that was blowing. She carried a small cane basket, which I had bought for her at one of the native shops just outside the gate in Fayid Village. Every morning she took this basket which carried her bottle of drink and some biscuits. I really was happy to see her so keen to go to school.

Norman had received three letters from Ian whilst Susan and I had been on the journey. They made me happy and sad at the same time. I was able to look at his photograph now without weeping. He seemed to have settled down, telling us in the letters about a play he was in and how he had joined the Scout Troop at the school. In every letter he mentioned that he was looking forward to joining us in the Christmas holidays, when all of us hoped that the children we had left behind would be brought out by the Army. With the political situation as it was, the prospect of the children being allowed to come to the Zone was becoming less and less likely, but we still lived in hope.

With the house put to rights, Norman at work and Susan at school I began to wonder what I was going to find to do. The servant we had, by the name of Mustafa, did all the cooking and cleaning. All there seemed for me to do was to go to the NAAFI to do the shopping.

The NAAFI building was very large; it had to be to house all the stock to support the Forces and families in the Zone. For our area it was just outside Kensington Village and near to Fayid Village, where only a few native shops were. Inside the building was one long counter where one queued for stores. There was little that one could not buy there, from meat and groceries to minerals, wine, beer, clothes, shoes etc. etc..

Fresh vegetables and fruit would be in short supply at times, then we would rely on an old man and his daughter who came around with their overladen donkey selling fresh eggs and vegetables. If things were really bad then a corvette or Royal Air Force planes would bring vegetables and fruit from Cyprus, but these supplies were dependent on the political situation and could not be relied upon.

There was no fresh milk to be had in the Zone. We existed entirely on tins of evaporated milk for our daily use. Evaporated milk if diluted to the consistency of fresh milk can be used for cooking and in beverages. There must have been a mountain of tinned milk housed in the NAAFI warehouses to supply everybody with their daily needs. If there was anything of importance wanted which was unobtainable from the NAAFI, then almost invariably there would be someone going into Ismailia on duty, who, if it were urgent, would bring back what was wanted.

The native shops sold large conical-shaped baskets; these were made from cane and were light in weight but very strong and had a strong handle. Most of the wives favoured these baskets because they held so much shopping. On a busy day the place seemed to be full of baskets. Armed guards patrolled the area for our protection.

With the shopping done I would sit and look out of my sitting room windows. All I could see was sand and more sand. "Oh dear!" I thought. "How ever am I going to settle down in this environment?" I need not have worried as in a very short time I became so busy that I then began to wonder how I was going to cope with all I had to do.

Susan and I had now been in the Canal Zone for three weeks. In this time the Troopship *The Empress of Australia*, on which our passage had originally been booked, had sailed from England and was now docked at Port Said. Norman came in with the most astonishing news about the ship. It had been allowed to dock but because of increasing hostilities the families on board were not allowed to disembark. The Troops were taken off because they were needed for reinforcements, but the families were to be sent back to the United Kingdom.

What a terrible disappointment for those wives and children, and the brides-to-be, who had come out to be married. The implications of it all were endless. My heart went out to all those mothers who had gone through so much upheaval, perhaps given up their homes and taken the children away from school and now were faced with having to return and pick up the pieces.

The NAAFI in Port Said, we heard, had opened its doors and allowed the wives and brides-to-be to spend one night with their menfolk on their premises, after the authorities had given permission for them to leave the ship for one night. What a bitter sweet night that must have been.

It made me shudder when I realised that that would have been the fate for Susan and me had we not had our passage switched and sailed on October 5th and not on October 25th.

I was not feeling too safe as it was. We had been told that the point system was being renewed and that many families would also be sent back to England. It was to be a "last out first home" situation. The reason being that the last out families would have their chance to come back again when the political situation improved.

I really tried to settle down after hearing this news. The next week I received a telephone call from a Brigadier's wife stationed in Moascar. Moascar was another large military station in the north part of the Zone, on the shores of Lake Timsah. It appeared that Norman had said at a cocktail party, that his wife was interested in the Girl Guide Movement and had been Guiding in India and South Africa, and of course at home in England. News like this travels fast and my phone call this day was to ask if she, the Brigadier's wife, could come to see me. She was the Division Commissioner of the Girl Guide Association for the whole of the Canal Zone. Little did I know what this phone call would lead me into!

We arranged a day for the Commissioner, Mrs Thompson, to come to lunch. Over the meal we chatted normally. It was a family lunch as Norman and Susan were at home. After lunch Mrs Thompson and I went into the sitting-room and over the coffee she asked me what experience I had had in Guiding. I was able to tell her that I had been Captain of Companies in India and South Africa and whilst at home in England I had been a very keen Guider and Local Association Member.

Then came the bombshell! "Right," she said, "you must become the District Commissioner for this area which comes under the heading of 'Canal South District'." She told me that she would be running the Canal North District as well as being the Division Commissioner for the whole Zone.

"Oh," was my reply, "I do not think I could take on such a high position." "You must," she said. She then began to explain at length that it was so important that the children in all the camps, Naval, Army and Royal Air Force, which were dotted all over the desert, isolated in their strictly guarded territories and surrounded by barbed wire, should be able to join in a movement that could keep them in contact with one another.

Guides, Brownies, Scouts and Cubs were doing this very job. The Companies and Packs, she told me, were there but they needed a leader at the top to keep them together and to encourage them. Visits to the stations would be necessary but I would be given a car and an armed escort for the journey. It all sounded very daunting but I felt I could not refuse and so, on this day I was appointed and contact was quickly made to Imperial Girl Guide Headquarters in London to send me my Warrant.

From then on I had no time to wonder what I was going to do with my time. There was the life I was to make with Norman in Army circles and the demanding job of becoming District Commissioner of Girl Guides. I had not yet met Norman's colleagues and their wives if they had accompanied their husbands. We needed to arrange cocktail parties and dinner parties.

I had not been introduced to the Officers' Club which was located on the shores of the Great Bitter Lake. It was not a busy time at the Club as we were in the cooler period of the year when cold winds put one off beach life. I was told that as soon as the hot weather came then the beach and waterfront life became very popular.

I had also found that we had the most charming neighbours. Their quarter joined on to ours but was separated by a high brick wall at the rear of the quarters. John was a Major in the Royal Welsh Fusiliers, and like Norman was stationed at GHQ. Mary, his wife, and two of their three children were with him, their elder son being left at home in England in boarding school. Mary and I could console one another on that point.

Army road block at the entrance to Kensington Village, Fayid

Aerial view of the family quarters in Kensington Village, Fayid

The front view of our quarter in Kensington Village

The rear view of our quarter in Kensington Village

The Lute caught in the Great Bitter Lake

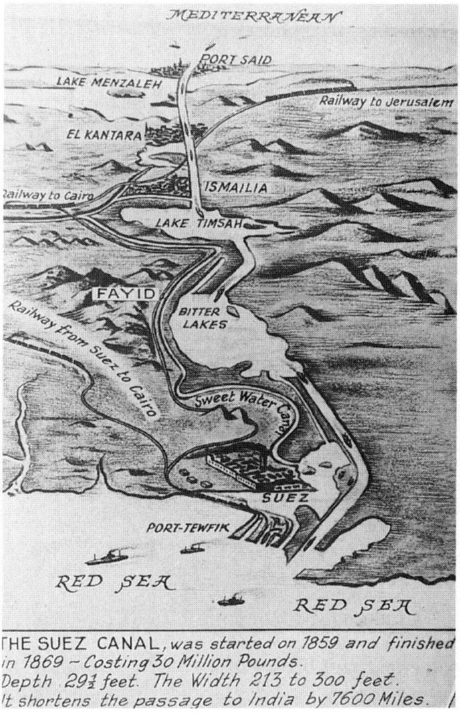

Aerial view of the area

The Avro York Aircraft chartered from Bovingdon to fly the school children from the UK to Nicosia, 1952

Saying farewell to Ian before the return flight, Nicosia, 1952

Brownie revels in the Major General's garden on the water front of The Great Bitter Lake

The Guiders enjoying their tea

Spectators at the Coronation Swimming Gala

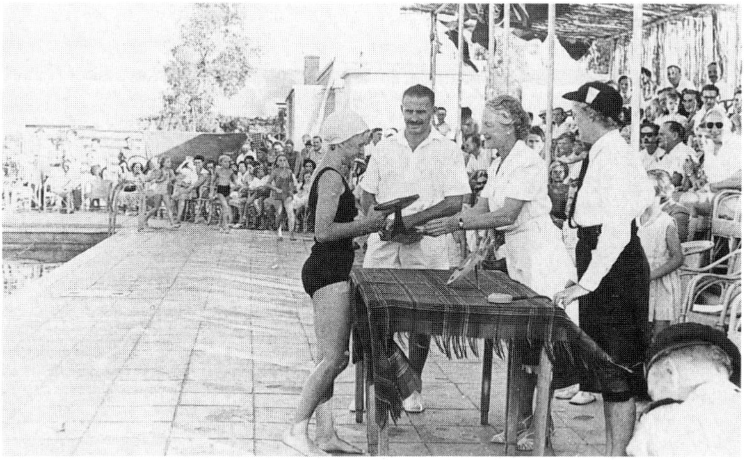

Presentation of trophies

The band of the 5th Royal Inniskilling Dragoon Guards who played at the coronation events

At a Boy Scout rally, Fayid, 1952

Scout and Guide commissioners at a rally in Fayid, 1952

March past of the Sea Rangers

Mary was a happy person, full of vitality and very practical. She and I became firm friends and John and Norman had a lot in common also. Their son, Ian, was the same age as Susan and attended the Army School. Susan and Ian would run along to school together. Anne, the little girl, was too young to go to school.

When the children came home, they each would go into their own houses, but it would not be long before we heard them calling to one another over the brick wall. It was quite amusing as Susan would sit one side of the wall and Ian and Anne the other. They would hold long conversations and throw little gifts over the wall. In the front gardens they would only have had a wire mesh separating them but as most of the daily life of the house took place on the back veranda, they much preferred the contact over the wall.

All the time the political situation was deteriorating and food supplies were becoming erratic. The suffragis, the Egyptian name for servants, were becoming surly and uncooperative.

John and Mary told us that they went fishing every weekend and the fish they caught helped tremendously with feeding the family. They asked us if we would like to join them and we were most enthusiastic.

Norman had brought his fishing rod and tackle out from England with him but I needed a rod also. He made me one from the aerial of a disused Army tank and we asked somebody to buy a reel, some line and hooks in Ismailia.

At the weekend John, Mary, Norman and I plus the three children, set off on our first fishing expedition together.

About six or seven miles along the canal road towards Suez was the Royal Air Force Station of Fanara. Outside the camp was Fanara Wharf and this is where we could fish.

The fish we caught was called 'lute' and it was like a medium-sized salmon. Occasionally one would catch a really large lute. It had white flesh when cooked and was a most welcome addition to the table. One fish would last two or three days as we asked the cook to prepare it in different ways.

It was exciting fishing as the fish would come in in great swirls and one would soon get a bite.

The children played as we fished. We could not stay long as there was a curfew on the road.

Invariably the wind would get up over the lake and it would become cold but if we came home with one or two large fish for the pot, we were well satisfied.

Three

British Girl Guides In Egypt

It was a shock when I received the registrations of the Girl Guide Companies and Packs. There were seven Guide Companies and eleven Brownie Packs. These were dotted all over the Zone as far flung as from Ismailia and Moascar in the north and Royal Air Force stations, both large and small, in the south towards Suez, whilst in the west they reached as far as Abu-Sueir and Tel-el-Kabir. This meant that a large number of girls of all ages were involved.

I knew then that I must start this job the very next day. I could well understand, from the papers I had before me, the urgency Mrs Thompson had impressed upon me.

I contacted the Guiders and invited as many as could travel safely to my house for a meeting. I found them all most enthusiastic and working hard in their Companies and Packs. I contacted the far-flung units and sent them messages of encouragement, telling them I would visit them as soon as the Army would allow me to travel.

I could visit most of the locations in my own car but to reach a few of the Royal Air Force Stations I was forced to have an Army vehicle with an armed escort to take me where I wanted to go.

There was one small RAF Station out towards Suez called Shallufa which had one Guider and four Brownies. The Brownies had passed their tenderfoot but could not be enrolled as their acting Brown Owl was not warranted. I quickly went out to the station and enrolled the Brownies whose faces beamed with satisfaction.

I sent to Alexandria for a Warrant for the Brown Owl and when next I went to present the Warrant, I found twelve Brownies in the Pack.

The County Commissioner for British Girl Guides in Egypt lived in Alexandria. She was a great help to me and would send mail and equipment through the 'Diplomatic Bag'. She visited us when she could but travel for her was not easy.

When I was Guiding in England the local Commissioner was a great believer in every town and village having a well run Local Association. "The Local Association is a body of representative people whose support leads to confidence in the soundness of the Movement on the part of parents and public, and whose function is to help Commissioners and Guiders with outside administration work and responsibilities." [Quoted from *Policy Organisation and Rules*.]

It is from a Local Association that one enlists badge testers and people with various skills who can instruct the Guides and Brownies in the subjects they wish to take to enable them to gain their badges.

A Local Association is also the greatest help with sports days, swimming galas, Brownie Revels and bazaars.

I realised that as soon as possible I must form a Local Association and have on it a representative from every station in the Zone, preferably the wife of the Commanding Officer or somebody he recommended.

Within the next two weeks I had visited the Commanding Officers of every station in my Zone except the outlying ones of Abu Sueir and Tel-el-Kabir; these I contacted by telephone and letter. They were all very helpful and very keen to have the children of the families in their stations occupied and happy.

Having received the names of willing people from the Commanding Officers, I then needed a President, Chairman, Secretary and Treasurer.

I approached Lady Robertson, the Major General's wife, at Flagstaff House and asked her if she would kindly be our President and she readily agreed. The wives of the other high ranking Officers were also helpful and enthusiastic.

The first meeting was held at Flagstaff House with Lady Robertson presiding.

I was much happier after this meeting and felt that I had enlisted the goodwill of the people around me. Unfortunately, just as I had all this under way, because of the hostilities and unrest the situation became most unstable. Many of the suffragis were becoming too frightened to come to work for the British. Every day fewer and fewer suffragis reported for work until one day they ceased to come altogether.

This meant a great deal of hardship for the families. The quarters were not equipped for easy running.

All the floors were tiled, likewise the verandas and outhouses. It was a large area which had to be swept every day and when the wind blew, which was often, the sand would blow into everything.

In the kitchens there was only a two burner oil Valor Perfection stove with an oven to put over the top of one burner and each kitchen possessed a primus stove. These were all the cooking facilities we had. We did, however, have electric kettles and coffee percolators in the house.

It was awful to be faced with the prospect of doing all the cooking, cleaning and shopping. Many of the wives were in tears.

Valor Perfection stoves were very temperamental and needed to be handled with care and precision. The oil wick if turned up a shade too high would cause black oily smuts to descend on to everything in the kitchen. When this happened then everything, walls as well, would have to be washed with hot soapy water. These stoves were the bane of our lives until we mastered them.

Norman came in one day with the news that the school children would not be allowed to come out from England for the Christmas holidays. This was a terrible blow and we found it very hard to have to write home to Ian and break the news to him. There were many families who had left their children behind in school and we had all hoped against hope that somehow the children would be flown out.

The Girl Guides came into their own during this crisis. In consultation with the Captains of the local Guide Companies, I decided it would be a help if the Guides were allowed to go around in pairs in their villages, never going outside the perimeter gates, to lend a hand to harassed mothers who really had more than their fair share to do. We put notices in the MI room and the Army school. If mothers needed help they could write down what help they needed and their name and address. In this way we could keep track of the Guides whilst they gave valuable assistance in many various ways. The Guides loved it and the help they gave was much appreciated.

Christmas was fast approaching. Mary and I began to plan, as we knew we would be entertaining some of the Officers whose wives were not with them.

We thought we really must make Christmas puddings. We rushed down to the NAAFI to buy the ingredients before the stocks ran out. This done we looked around out kitchens for bowls large enough in which to make our mixtures. We could find nothing large enough until we spied, both in her kitchen and mine, two "Pots, Chamber, Officers for the use of", sitting on a top shelf still in their original wrappings, never having been used.

With much laughter we took them down, unwrapped them, gave them a good wash and commenced to make our mixture in them. The families came in to 'stir for luck' just as was the custom way back home. We had been issued with a two tier steamer which could be put over one of the burners of the oil stove. Whilst the puddings steamed for hours there was constant checking of the oil burners.

Everybody was determined not to let the political situation spoil the festivities of Christmas.

The garrison church which was inside Kensington Village, was decorated beautifully. Padre Druitt, the Chaplain, was a charming man, very good with the troops and he was also excellent with the children. His Sunday School was always well attended.

He gave a service for the children just before Christmas. He was telling them the Christmas story and how the wise men and the shepherds travelled across the desert following the star until they came to the place where the baby Jesus lay, when a small boy put up his hand and said "Please Sir, why did they not fall over the barbed wire?" How poignant it is that a young boy should be so used to the barbed wire that he thought it had always been there.

The weather over Christmas was perfect, bright sunshine with a gentle cool breeze.

On Christmas Day I cooked dinner for ten people. We invited Susan's headmistress from the Army school and five unattached Officers.

Because I had to concentrate on the intricate timing to get the oil stove, the primus plus the steamer, to do what I wanted, the dinner turned out to be one of the finest I have ever cooked.

It was a lovely happy Christmas but my heart ached when I thought of Ian and I hated the fact that he was not there with us.

There soon started a large evacuation of families back to the United Kingdom. Families were being brought into the safe area from Ismailia, Abu Sueir and Tel-el-Kabir, and Army personnel who were living in private accommodation on the shores of the Great Bitter Lake were brought in also. It meant we all had to double up and take a family into our quarters. We had a young Major, his wife and small baby from the REME depot in Tel-el-Kabir. The Major stayed only a few days as he had to report back for duty. We cared for his wife and baby until they were notified of a place on a troopship.

It was sad to see the families go; some had only been in the Zone a short time. The strategy behind sending the last out families home was that in a three year posting they would be able to return when the political situation became stable again.

I was showing signs of strain with all the work there was to do and no suffragi to help. Norman said he would apply for a batman – at least he would take the sweeping off me and could clean the shoes, etc..

The batman he brought along was a real character. His family were bargees and Atkins, which was his name, was born on a barge. He was a real toughie but likeable and willing. He turned up for work one day with a black eye. I asked him how he came by it. He said, "That's the one I didn't miss!" Once he was absent for three days. This was because he had been put in solitary confinement for fighting. I liked him and he certainly was a help.

Mary came in one day and told me that she and the children were on the list to return to the UK. This was awful news. We had been such friends and had had a lot of fun together. Susan was going to miss the children.

Mary had three chickens which she kept in a wire mesh run at the back of her quarter. They had given her about ten eggs a week and she found this excellent in that she was able to give the children fresh eggs for breakfast or tea. Mary asked me if I would like to have the chickens when she left. I was very keen to have them; I enlisted Atkins' help in making a run in our back garden and I put the nesting boxes in it. Now we had to catch the chickens to bring them from Mary's garden into mine. I have never seen anything so hilarious as Atkins trying to catch these chickens. He was a large fellow and six feet tall. The chickens escaped him at every turn. The swearing he did, when he thought he had one in his grasp only to land face downwards in the sand with the chicken running off in another direction, was the language only a bargee could use.

After a lot of cursing and swearing from Atkins, we finally got the chickens into the run.

Egyptian chickens are not a bit like English chickens. To begin with they stand up to lay their eggs. Being enthusiastic to look after these chickens I put straw in their nesting boxes, thinking they would be nice and comfortable. They would have none of it and scratched and scratched until they had removed it all. I remembered an aunt of mine who kept chickens, boiling up potato peelings and making them a nice mash. I made mash and found a kind of trough in which to put it. This caused havoc. They would not eat the mash from the trough but commenced cackling and scratching until they had turned it all out on to the sand. When it was on the sand, then they would eat it. They were obviously not used to luxury. However when they settled down they supplied me with nine or ten eggs a week; that was if the eggs were not cracked in the process of being laid whilst the chicken stood up to lay them.

The day came when Mary and the children were to leave for their journey home to the UK. Mary brought the children round to say goodbye. I had never seen the children so clean and tidy before. Ian was dressed in a pair of shorts and a white shirt with a very smart bow tie. Anne had her hair beautifully brushed and combed and was wearing a pretty white dress. They looked like two little angels. Anne gave a cough and I said to her, "Oh Anne, have you got a cold?" "No," she said, "I've dot a toff."

It was indeed a sad day for all of us.

In the month of March the Khamsin arrives. A Khamsin is a very high wind which blows on and off for fifty days. The word 'Khamsin' comes from the Arabic meaning 'fifty'.

It is the most awful time of year. The wind blows so hard that sandstorms ensue. The sandstorms can last for three or four days. The days are like night. The atmosphere is like a thick fog and the sand blows into everything.

It was a constant battle to keep free of the sand and I was very thankful to have the batman, Atkins, to help with the sweeping.

It was a dreary time of the year.

I thought a lot about the Girl Guides and the Brownies and indeed about all the children in the Zone, living as they were under restrictions and encircled by barbed wire.

In the smaller stations there would not be an Army school, in that case the children would be collected in an Army bus with armed guards on board with another bus following also with armed guards, and taken to the nearest station where there was a school.

I thought about devising a competition for the Girl Guides and Brownies to take part in, and then changed my mind as I sat listening to the Radio, broadcasting from our "Forces Broadcasting Service Canal Zone".

The programme to which I was listening was of topical items submitted by people in the Zone.

'Why,' I thought to myself, 'can't the Guides and Brownies have a slot in the programme?'

Each Company and Pack could go on the air for a short time once a week. This would create a lot of interest and the girls would have to work at it to be ready with a programme when it was their turn.

The next morning I went off to visit the Officer in Charge at the Forces Broadcasting Service. He was delighted with the idea and suggested that twenty minutes would be long enough.

When I approached the Guiders they all welcomed the extra impetus it would give.

Everybody started work at once to get their programmes ready and they were to let me know which weeks they preferred.

Soon I was able to present a rota of Companies and Packs to the Broadcasting Officer and a date was fixed to commence.

It was a commitment and it was very good training for the girls as they were committed to the dates they had chosen and there was no getting out of it.

It was just the thing to keep the Companies and Packs in contact with one another, and it would take many weeks before all the units had had their turn.

The Brownies when they were on the air were a delight with their chatter, and a few giggles, when they told us what they had been doing and who had gained her 'Golden Bar' or what badges they had worked for and achieved. They usually gave a song and finished with their Fairy Ring.

Amongst the Guides there were some very good voices and their Camp Fire Songs were a delight to listen to. Most people were surprised at the high standards they achieved when they broadcast.

When the troubles started in the Canal Zone in the autumn of 1951, it was necessary to send to Cyprus and Tripoli for reinforcements of troops. No. 2 Brigade at Cyprus came over with Infantry, Gunners, Field Ambulances and REME Workshops. This new contingent was based at El Ballah and El Kirsh, both further along from Fayid towards Suez.

Force's families were living in Cyprus at Larnaca, Famagusta and Nicosia. When their menfolk were over in the Canal Zone, the families were on their own and the wives found it a lonely existence. They agitated to be allowed to visit their husbands. They were soon called 'The Abandoned Wives of Cyprus'. This prompted the authorities to devise a scheme whereby visits could be made. The scheme, when devised, allowed the wives to visit the Canal Zone for a period of fifty-nine days, after which time they were to return to Cyprus. They could only visit if they were sponsored by a family already in the Zone who were willing to house them whilst they were there. It also depended on them being able to obtain a passage on one of the few corvettes that were used to bring supplies across from Cyprus.

A REME Major had come across with No. 2 Brigade and was now commanding the workshops at El Ballah as the D.A.E.M.E.. Norman and he had served together in Calcutta and we were very pleased to see him now that he was so near to us. We were very happy to sponsor his wife, Helen, whom we had met in England at one of the Corps Balls held each summer at the REME Headquarters in Arborfield.

Helen came over and she divided her time between us and some Royal Air Force friends of theirs who were stationed at Kabrit. This was nearer El Ballah and more convenient for Tom, her husband, to visit. It seemed so hard that we should have to say farewell to Helen at the end of her stay and send her back like all the other 'abandoned wives' from Cyprus when their visit time expired.

It was now Easter. We had attended a lovely Easter Day service at the garrison church which was filled to capacity.

When we arrived home we found a charming young woman on our veranda waiting for our return. She was wearing such a pretty hat and when I remarked how pretty it was, she, with a smile, said it was her "Easter Bonnet". She had called as she had heard that I was the Girl Guide Commissioner.

We asked her to join us in a pre-lunch drink. Over the drinks it was revealed that she had had a lot of experience in the Guiding world and she had come along this morning to see if she could help me. This was like music to my ears as there were many girls of sixteen and over in the Fayid area and I had nobody to form a Ranger Company.

When in England she and her family lived in Hayling Island where they berthed the yacht they owned. All the family were enthusiastic sailors. Hearing all this I ventured to ask her if she would form and run a Sea Ranger Company. Her eyes lit up and, smiling sweetly, she said she would be delighted to do so.

Her name was Nina and she lived in another village, not far over the sand, called Gibraltar Village. This village had not long been built and now housed many forces families. Nina's husband was a Major in the Royal Signals. They had two children, a boy and a girl. The daughter was with them but the son, who was the eldest, was at home in boarding school.

Over the weeks Nina not only proved to be an excellent Guider but she and I have kept up a life-long friendship and it all started on that Easter Day.

Norman said we should go to the beach on the shore of the Great Bitter Lake in the afternoon. The warmer weather was on its way and the hot season would soon follow. This is when the waterfront would be crowded with people trying to keep cool.

A colleague of Norman's, whose family had returned to the UK, was wanting to pass on to us a beach hut that he was no longer using and if we liked it we could have it for our use.

The beach was very sandy and stretched the length of the Great Bitter Lake. The beach had marked separate areas for Officers, Non-Commissioned Officers and Troops, and each area had its own club house.

We first enrolled as members of the Officers' Club for the season and then went to look for the beach hut. It was in a good position a little way from the Club House but in sight of the jetty. The jetty was long enough to provide a pleasant walk out over the Lake.

We liked the hut and thought its awning would provide shelter from the sun when the weather was hot. There was also a flat-bottomed boat in the hut. It had canvas sides over a light wooden frame. Wooden slats were on the bottom supporting two wooden seats. A thin band of wood went right round the middle on the outside of the canvas and a wooden rail supported the top with rollocks and two oars. The bow was nicely shaped and the stern was strong and upright.

Norman said if we could buy this boat he would then write home to his father to ask him to ship out to us an outboard motor. This he could clip on to the stern of the boat thus allowing us to take it out into the deeper and cleaner water where we could go over the side of the boat to swim.

Susan thought this a wonderful idea as she loved water and was a good little swimmer. We all hoped Norman's friend would sell us the boat. We could not wait until the next day for the answer, so we went into the Club to phone him. The answer was "Yes!"

The whole day had been special. It had started at breakfast time when we had eggs that Norman had painted with an Easter theme and which had been laid by our own chickens. The

NAAFI had not risen to chocolate Easter Eggs! Added to this we were now proud owners of a beach hut and a boat and I had acquired a Sea Ranger Captain!

The months were slipping by and the mothers who had left their older children at home in boarding school were grieving for them and becoming restless. Going around as I did with my Guiding work I met many of them.

We had heard that the Earl and Countess Mountbatten of Burma were to pay a visit to the Troops in the Canal Zone.

This set us all thinking. We knew what a dynamic personality the Countess was and how she got things moving wherever she went. We began to think that perhaps she would help us to have the school children flown out to us for the summer holidays. We could stress to her that it was impossible, because of the restrictions, for us to travel home to our children. If we did so we would not be allowed back into the Zone again. We were in a very unhappy situation, torn between our children and our husbands.

I let it be known that I would hold a meeting of all mothers involved if they came to my house for coffee on a certain morning. There were approximately twenty mothers at that meeting. It was decided that I should write a letter of petition to Edwina, Countess Mountbatten of Burma, and enclose a list of their signatures.

I had spoken of this letter I was about to write, to Mrs Thompson, the Division Commissioner of Girl Guides, who lived in Moascar. She said I should also write to the Brigadier in charge of Administration for British Troops in Egypt, telling him I had written to the Countess and my reason for doing so. I sent the two letters to arrive a few days before the Mountbattens were expected.

On the day of their arrival there was an evening reception and dinner at the Headquarters of M.E.L.F. (Middle East Land Forces). The General was the host. His wife had not accompanied him on his tour so he asked Mrs Thompson, who was a Brigadier's wife, to act as hostess in her place.

The General and Mrs Thompson were standing at the top of the staircase in readiness to greet the Earl and Countess. As Edwina reached the top step and shook the General's hand, she was heard to say, "What's this nonsense about the school children not coming out; of course they are, you had better see to it."

No more was said on the subject. Edwina had made her point and that was that!

The next morning Mrs Thompson phoned me and said, "It worked!" and told me how the evening progressed.

The mothers and fathers were overjoyed with the result but we all knew we had a long way to go before matters would be finalised.

There was no sign of the suffragis coming back to work.

Atkins had been a great help to me, but now he was to move on with his Unit to another base. I would miss him, he had been such a character; tough, but likeable.

Norman said he would apply for another batman. He brought along a young soldier of about nineteen years of age, different in every way from Atkins. He was small-framed, not shy but meek and mild. His name was Holdsworth and he came from Yorkshire. I was told he was to live on the premises and I could well see why, barrack life would have been much too harsh for him.

I had to rush around and make the room in the compound comfortable for him. The Quarter Master Stores supplied me with furniture and bedding for him.

Holdsworth soon settled down and seemed happy to be living with us.

Susan, as the saying goes, could 'twist him around her little finger'. She loved skipping and would say to Holdsworth, "Please help me turn my skipping rope." They would tie the end of the rope on to a hook in the veranda wall and Holdsworth was to turn the other end. Soon I would hear Susan say, "Salt, mustard, vinegar, pepper, faster, Holdsworth, faster!" I never interfered as they seemed to enjoy this pastime.

One evening I was wondering what I could cook for supper when I remembered that macaroni cheese was a pleasant dish. It was all right until I wanted to grill the grated cheese I had put on the top. There was no form of grill in our kitchens. I used all my ingenuity to rig up a grill. We had a small electric fire which had two elements of coiled wire on the front. I took this into the pantry where there was a stone shelf. I placed two piles of three bricks each on the shelf and rested the electric fire face downwards across the top of the piles of bricks leaving sufficient room for me to slide my pie dish underneath. It was marvellous and browned the cheese topping beautifully.

I left a portion of macaroni cheese in the kitchen for Holdsworth and took the rest into the house for our supper. We thoroughly enjoyed ours. Later I went into the kitchen and asked Holdsworth if he had enjoyed his. "Oh, Mum!" [I had tried so hard to teach him to say 'Ma'am', but it always came out as 'Mum'.] He said, "Oh, Mum, it fair made me fetch!" Poor Holdsworth, he would much rather have had a "chip butty".

One morning I had taken our little Fiat car along the Canal Road on my way to visit a Girl Guide Captain who was a physiotherapist working at the British Military Hospital. On the return journey I saw a market which had been set up just back from the side of the road. I was thinking it would be nice if I could buy some fresh vegetables.

I stopped my car, locking the doors before I left it and walked the short distance to the market.

I bought the vegetables and was just turning to go back to my car when a bunch of Egyptians surrounded me. They were all talking at once and were very excited about something. They kept saying, "You want it taxi, lady, you want it taxi." "No!" I said, "I do not want a taxi, I have my own car. Please let me pass."

With great relief I saw they were quietening down and I began to walk towards my car.

It was then that I saw what all the commotion had been about. They had surrounded me so that I could not see them stealing my car. What was I to do now with no car in which to drive home?

It was fortunate that I was on the Canal Road where the Services vehicles plied up and down.

I waved the first Army truck to stop, but no luck, they did not want to know. I waved another, still no response, I was getting desperate.

The next vehicle to come along was a Royal Navy truck. The driver kindly stopped and after my telling him that I was stranded he helped me into his cab. I needed the help as the steps up into it were very high.

I asked him to take me to the E.M.E. Directorate where Norman worked. I went through the office door and the Major said, "Sorry, but the Colonel is away at a meeting."

There were about six people in the office and their faces dropped as I told them my story, they were concerned for me, wondering what Norman would say.

They took me home and feeling miserable I waited for Norman's return.

I heard afterwards that as Norman came out of the office to come home they had said to him, "Let her down lightly, sir."

To my great relief all Norman said when he came in was, "Well, I'll have to go to Cyprus to fetch a new one." Norman was always marvellous on big issues, it was the smaller ones he made a fuss about.

I was really sad at losing our dear little Fiat, Norman had bought it especially to meet Susan and me when we docked at Port Said.

This incident started a spate of car thefts. Many more people suffered my fate. If they did not lose their car, they would find it minus its wheels.

It was going to be difficult for me without the use of our car and it would be a few weeks before a new one could be sent over from Cyprus. Norman said he would go across to Cyprus as soon as possible to order a new one.

At the last meeting of the Girl Guide Captains and the Brown Owls it was decided that we would organise 'Brownie Revels' for the Brownies and a swimming gala for the Girl Guides, with a few items of easy swimming inserted into the programme for the Brownies.

These two events would entail a great deal of coordination and without my own transport it was going to be a strain. I could order an official car for long journeys, but for running around the Fayid area this would not be practical.

I held a meeting of the Local Association at Flagstaff House.

It was a very good meeting. Everybody was very enthusiastic and I was offered a lot of help and support for both events.

I told the members that we hoped to invite the Brownies of the Canal North District to the Revels and if they were able to come, (always there was the worry that restrictions on travel would be enforced on the very day we had arranged the Revels), there would be approximately a hundred Brownies.

We also hoped the Division Commissioner would attend.

A large area would have to be found to accommodate such a large number.

At once a Major-General's wife very kindly offered us her garden. It was large and faced the waterfront of the Great Bitter Lake.

By the time the meeting came to a close I was most gratified that every member had volunteered to help in one way or another. If they did not do the job themselves then a promise was made that they would find the right person to do the job.

For instance, for the swimming gala we would need judges, time keepers, recorders, starters, life-savers and a clerk of the Bath.

The Guides and Brownies had made very good use of the swimming season. Organised practices were held each week at the Olympia Pool, Fayid.

The Army Physical Training Corps very kindly sent along an instructor from the Corps each week. Consequently, by the time we put on the gala the standard of the swimming and diving was very high.

The Brownie Revels were a delight; the mothers helped with the tea and each Pack with their Brown Owl and Tawny Owl found its own home in the garden and came together for games and their Fairy Ring and Grand Howl.

These two events promoted a lot of goodwill and happiness, and everybody seemed to be involved. It boosted morale, which was needed when living under a cloud of political unrest.

Four

The Arrival Of The Children

It did not come as a surprise when communiqués from Headquarters in Moascar were sent to all Stations, asking parents who wished their children to be flown out from the UK for the summer holidays to send in names and details of the children and the names and addresses of their guardians in the UK.

I had received an acknowledgement of the letter I had sent to Edwina Countess Mountbatten of Burma, from her Secretary, with a message from the Countess saying that she hoped to be able to help us. Now, with the arrival of the communiqués, things seemed to be moving and there was a feeling of optimism instead of the spirit of pessimism which had previously prevailed.

Soon after this event I received through the E.M.E. Directorate a letter from the Brigadier in charge of families, asking me if I would go into Moascar to see him.

The Commanding Officer of RAF Abyad, who wished to have his three children flown out to him said, if I wished, he would take me into Moascar in his staff car.

I was pleased to have his support and he was pleased to give it. The youngest of his three children was only six years old. His wife had not accompanied him on his tour and it was going to be a big undertaking for him to look after his three children, if they came.

On the appointed day Leigh, the RAF CO, with his staff car and driver called at our house and we set off for Moascar.

I had not been out of the Fayid area for some time and it was a pleasant ride along the road with the Sweet Water Canal on the one side and the Great Bitter Lake on the other. It was difficult to realise that the political situation was so strained and the peace so fragile when the scenes on the side of the road were so peaceful and picturesque.

The fellahin were toiling in the small oases of vegetation and date palms. Goat herds were tended by women and children. The women wore long black flowing robes and veils with heavy metal adornments on their arms and ankles, large earrings and some wearing yashmaks. There were overladen donkeys, water buffalo and camels here and there. The native felluca, with its characteristic lateen rigging, which to my mind looks as if the sails are upside down when in reality it is a triangular sail, has a long yard and a short mast with the sail rigged to the mast at an angle of forty-five degrees. These vessels are very picturesque, sailing lazily on the water. The felluca is very much a feature of the Eastern Mediterranean. As we sped by car towards Moascar these scenes gave us a false sense of security.

The driver of the car found his way to the Brigadier's office and we arrived on time. I was a little apprehensive as I went in as I had not been told the reason for my visit.

The Brigadier was charming and put me at my ease very quickly, coffee was sent for, and he was soon telling me why he had asked me to come to see him. It was, of course, about the school children coming out for the summer holidays.

It appeared that after receiving the filled-in application forms from the parents who wished their children to come out, the total was thirty-two children, ranging in ages from six to sixteen, and there were, it seemed, as many boys as girls.

The Brigadier said that he would be able to organise the travelling out and the return travel. He was planning to have the children flown out from the UK by chartered plane which would land at Nicosia airport in Cyprus. They would be met there and brought over from Cyprus to Fayid by ship. The ship they would use would be *The Charlton Star*. This ship was in service to take Army personnel backwards and forwards to the Army camps set up in Cyprus to accommodate troops and families when they went on leave.

The travel arrangements the Brigadier said he could organise without difficulty but he would need assistance when the thirty-two children arrived.

As I was working with children of all ages as the Girl Guide Commissioner he thought that I would be the best person to ask for this help.

He suggested that I asked another mother and two fathers to help me and we could work as a team.

The plan was that the two mothers, one of them myself, and two fathers would go over on *The Charlton Star* the day before the children were due to arrive. Accommodation in a hotel would be booked for the four of us for the first night. We were to contact an Agent who would reserve sufficient hotel accommodation for the second night for the thirty-two children and the four adults. The children would be in need of a night's rest after their journey by plane and before we all embarked on *The Charlton Star* the next day.

I felt with the help of three other people and the Brigadier's organisation I would be able to undertake this responsibility.

The Brigadier seemed pleased, as I left his office, at the outcome of our meeting.

On the return journey to Fayid I was telling Leigh all that had transpired. He said at once that he would be one father and he felt sure that his second in command, a Wing Commander, by the name of Richard, would volunteer to be the second father. He would ask him when he returned home and let me know his answer.

When I arrived in Kensington Village I went straight across the road from our quarter to a quarter of a friend of mine, another Colonel's wife. Her name was Jill. She had a daughter on the list and she was very pleased to volunteer to be the second mother.

The next morning I made contact with the Brigadier by telephone. He was pleased all was well my end and that I could give him the names of the three volunteers, the Wing Commander having agreed. I rang off saying I would wait further instructions.

The guardians of the children in the UK, whether they were grandparents, aunts or uncles, or friends of the family would be briefed by the Army authorities in London with details of the chartered plane, the airport and time of departure. The excitement of the children would be very great.

In the Canal Zone the mothers, fathers, brothers and sisters of the thirty-two children were overjoyed at the prospect of the families being re-united in a very short time now.

None of us knew that the political situation was becoming ugly again.

Just ten days before the date of the children's departure from London all hell was let loose. News came that the political situation was very unstable with nerves stretched to the limit on both sides.

In order to keep the peace, the ship, *The Charlton Star* (which was to transport the children from Cyprus to Fayid) was commandeered by the Military and sent to Tripoli and Benghazi for reinforcements of troops.

Then the Government in Cyprus became so nervous that it announced a clamp down on all civilian aircraft landing at Nicosia airport.

What a state of affairs!

The air was 'hot' with cables and wireless messages being sent backwards and forwards from the UK and Cyprus to Moascar and Fayid. Desperately the parents of the children were trying to send cables to the guardians in the UK to ensure that they kept in contact with the Army authorities for news of developments and for new instructions.

We knew what anxiety it must be for those caring for the children and we were truly sorry to cause them so much trouble.

To everyone's great relief the Royal Air Force came to the rescue. A Royal Air Force plane was chartered from Bovingdon Aerodrome in Hertfordshire and, because it was not a civilian plane, it would be allowed to land in Cyprus.

So far so good, but there was the question of how the children were to be transported from Cyprus to Fayid without the ship to carry them.

In the nick of time a solution was found. RAF Fayid was to supply two planes. They would fly over to Nicosia airport the day before the children were due to arrive and take the two mums and the two dads with them. The planes would wait and fly back two days later with the children and the four of us on board.

We could only hope that the Army authorities had briefed all the guardians with their new instructions, and that all would be well in the end.

The day came when all this organisation came into operation.

Leigh, Richard, Jill and I were driven to RAF Fayid where we boarded one of the two planes that were to take us to Cyprus.

Early evening saw us settled in a very good hotel in which accommodation had been booked for us. We had taken a walk around the town of Nicosia and found it strange walking down tree-lined streets passing houses, shops and restaurants on the way.

It was pleasant to sit chatting over dinner that evening. A sense of freedom came over us away from the restrictive life we were living in the Canal Zone.

Although we had our clubs and we entertained a lot ourselves it was all confined within our own immediate circles and behind barbed wire.

We were enjoying this sense of freedom sitting over our after dinner coffee and liqueurs in the lounge of the hotel when the Agent we were to contact the next morning came into the hotel to introduce himself.

He said he was pleased to see us relaxing as he thought we would have a busy time on the morrow.

He told us that he would be bringing the list of the names and details of the children to us in the morning, together with the names of the hotels and the amount of accommodation each one could give us. Then we would have to work out where to put the children. He said he thought it would be quite a task.

This dampened our spirits a bit and made us retire to our beds not too late.

I did not sleep well as the night was hot and I was far too excited at the thought of seeing Ian and the other children the next day.

We were all up fairly early in the morning and waited for the Agent.

When we received the lists we sat in the grounds of the hotel underneath an awning and began our task. As the morning drew on it became hotter and hotter, and soon we were pleased to find a cool spot inside the hotel.

There were four hotels on our list, each one giving us a varying number of beds.

With paper and pencils we worked through the morning. First we would put it this way, then scrap what we had done and start all over again.

By lunch time we thought we had it right, when we found we had a sixteen year old boy in a bedroom with a fourteen year old girl. We unscrambled everything and began on another plan.

In the end, as I had a son I took eleven more boys and went into a hotel that gave us thirteen beds. Jill had a daughter and so took seven more girls. Leigh with his three children we placed in another hotel with six more children. Richard took the residue and finally we had a plan that worked. The Agent had been right, it had been a task.

Now we were to go out to the airfield to establish our arrival and make ourselves known, and on the way back we would call into the hotels to check that everything was in order.

We reported to the Military at the airport and were briefed about the plane carrying the children. We did not know until that moment that the aircraft chartered from Bovingdon was an Avro York and had been converted from a Lancaster Bomber. It had four piston engines and its speed was 204 miles per hour. Any speed over 210 put too much strain on the wings. It had a drooping belly and was a heavy craft. Because of its limited fuel-carrying capacity it could not do the journey in one hop and had broken its journey at Malta, arriving there at midday. The latest news was that it had left Malta and estimating its speed it could not arrive until very late evening.

We would have to wait to hear from the children all the other details of the journey.

We were advised to arrive at the airport at about 9.30 p.m. when more news would be available.

We felt for the children as it was such a long journey with very little comfort – how tired they would be.

The waiting time for us seemed endless. 9.30 p.m. seemed as if it would never come.

When we finally arrived at the airport we were jollied along by the staff, who supplied us with cool drinks and generally chatted.

They told us the plane was not making very good time and could not possibly arrive until around midnight. We were all very anxious, Jill and I particularly. The two men were airmen themselves and viewed all this delay from a different aspect.

About 11.30 p.m. we were invited to go up into the control tower where we could watch for the plane to arrive.

Some minutes before midnight one of the Officers said, "I am in contact with the plane. Would you like to talk to the children?" We thought about it and decided that it was best not to talk to them. The strain for us would have been too much and we thought it would upset the children.

Presently the Officer said, "Look over to your left at an angle of 2 o'clock and you will see the lights of the plane flashing."

It was an emotional moment as we watched the plane come out of a black sky knowing it was full of the children, ours amongst them. It came in with a bumpy landing and taxied to the exit.

We rushed down to the exit area which was surrounded by a wire mesh fence with gates.

The search lights were on and we watched the children tumble out of the craft. They looked dazed, as I am sure they must have been after such a long journey.

I saw Ian and went to run to the wire fence when Leigh caught hold of my arm and said I should not attract Ian's attention until I could hold him. I am afraid I was not strong enough to hold back and ran to the fence and called him. He came running and there we were, we could only squeeze our fingers through the mesh to make contact. Through my tears of joy I told him I had all the children to look after and I would meet him when he passed through the gate, and when we reached the hotel we could say a real hello.

Both my children have been very good at understanding when mummy had a job to do. They had been taught that they must wait and when I had finished the job, then their turn would come. Army life teaches all members of the family a discipline.

We assembled the children and counted heads, and to our great relief, there were thirty-two.

Buses were waiting to take them to their hotels.

Arrangements had been made for sandwiches, milk and cool drinks to be served at each hotel.

I showed each one of my eleven boys into their rooms and told them I would be around again to say goodnight.

I tucked each one in making sure they did not have too many clothes on as the night was hot. They had travelled mostly in their school uniforms and these were thick. They had needed the thick clothes in the plane as it became very cold. Blankets were given to them, but these were mainly used to keep rain off when it leaked through the skin of the aircraft.

I was saying goodnight to one small boy who I could tell came from the East End of London, as he had a lovely cockney accent. He was wearing a thick fleecy-lined vest with short sleeves and I suggested that he would be more comfortable if he took off his thick vest and just used the sheet to cover him up. He looked quite affronted and said, "Me and my vest can't be parted."

I got back to the room I was sharing with Ian who was already in bed and nearly asleep. It was then I could hug and kiss him and the smile on his face was enough reward for all the anxieties we had been through to achieve this moment.

It was an early rise for the two mums and the two dads. They had to make sure that the children in their charge were up and dressed with their suitcases packed and deposited downstairs in the foyers of their hotels before breakfast.

The children were looking better after their night's sleep, short though it was. When they came off the plane the night before they had white faces and black rings around their eyes. No wonder as the journey had been long and arduous.

Over breakfast my twelve little boys were eager to tell me about their journey. Ian had told me quite a bit also.

Most of the children, Ian being one of them, had congregated at a point in Goodge Street, near Tottenham Court Road, in London in the afternoon of the day before the journey. They had been met by the Army authorities and taken by coach to Bovingdon Aerodrome. They were housed overnight in the barracks on the airfield in order for an early start in the morning.

Only a few who lived near enough to be able to travel by car went independently to Bovingdon. Leigh's three children were taken by their mother. They lived at Northwood in Middlesex. They had to leave home before 4 a.m. to reach Bovingdon at 5 a.m.. The plane was airborne as soon as possible after sunrise.

The aircraft came down into Malta to refuel and the children were given lunch in the airport. They landed in the heat of midday which was very hot indeed.

The boys were telling me that they were either too hot or too cold.

When they were once more in the plane and travelling through the night it became very cold. Blankets were issued to keep them warm. Rain seeped through the roof of the craft and blankets were rigged up to keep the children dry.

The engines were noisy and the chatter of thirty-two children was excessive.

I received complaints from all sides as the stories came tumbling out. Food was issued in paper bags but there was plenty to drink on board.

It was interesting to hear the boys talk. In spite of the grumbles I could sense they were enjoying themselves, and when one came to think about it, it must have been a great adventure for them.

11 a.m. saw us all assembled on the airfield at Nicosia with the two planes from RAF Fayid waiting for us. After survival drill we boarded the planes and were off.

There was great excitement as we touched down at RAF Fayid. The children left their seats, picked up their baggage and were ready to stampede off the aeroplane. There was one mum and one dad on each plane and it was necessary to wait a few minutes until they quietened down before we could open the doors and let them off in an orderly fashion.

The parents were almost as bad as the children in their eagerness to reach their offspring. It was a scene of laughter and tears as the families were reunited.

Norman and Susan were there to greet Ian, it was lovely to see them together. They took him home whilst we four adults thanked the pilots and their crew members and generally finished the job.

It had been a mission well worth while and we felt a warm sense of satisfaction that all had gone so well.

I phoned the Brigadier and told him "mission accomplished". He gave a big sigh of relief and congratulated us.

It was wonderful when I finally reached home to find Ian there with Susan rushing around trying to show him everything at once. The home seemed complete and we could look forward to six weeks of holidays before Ian, with the rest of the children, would go back to the United Kingdom again.

Five

The Hot Weather Season

The hot weather really was with us now. To avoid the heat of the day the menfolk started work at 7 a.m. and finished for the day at lunch time. The temperatures would soar to the hundreds and when it was 105 in the shade it was pretty uncomfortable. Fortunately we could go to the beach where we could swim to keep cool.

As soon as lunch was over we would pack what gear we needed and off we would go to the beach. Luckily the outboard motor for the boat, which Norman's father had had shipped out to us, had arrived. The new car from Cyprus had arrived also.

Ian was very impressed with the beach and the lake and ecstatic about the boat and the beach hut.

The outboard motor was taken to the beach with us every day in the boot of the car. It would not have been safe to leave it in the hut.

In our swim suits, but well-covered against the sun with sun-hats and long-sleeved shirts, we did our boating.

Norman would clip the motor on to the stern of the boat and out we would go into the deep clear water. Near the shore the water was not very clean but as soon as we went further out into the lake the water became a lovely clear bluey-green.

We had a small ladder which we would lower down over the side of the boat to enable us to let ourselves down into the water. The children just slipped off the side of the boat. When trying to get back into the boat the ladder was a great help. It was never very easy to get back into the boat again.

Either Norman or I would stay in the boat, taking it in turns to swim, so as to keep the boat near the children when they swam.

By the time we had returned to the shore it was time for our picnic tea and a rest under the awning of the beach hut. We would sit and watch the lake, waiting for the breeze to come wafting across the water.

Every afternoon when the sun went down and the temperature dropped one would see ripples coming across the water followed by the breeze.

This was our relief from the heat of the day. The wind in the desert can be a blessing but can also be an annoyance. In order to try to keep as cool as possible all the doors and windows are left open, then the wind really whistles through the house taking any paperwork one might be attending to with it.

Club life was in full swing now. One could either stay on one's own corner of the beach or go into the Club to meet people.

Leigh would come over from Abyad with his three children. He said one afternoon that he thought of planning a boat trip across the Great Bitter Lake, landing on the shore at the other side in the Sinai Desert. He wondered if we would like to join him and he would ask a few other families to make up a party.

We thought this a wonderful idea and thought it would be an exciting day out for the children.

Leigh arranged it all. He was able to hire an RAF Launch for the day, together with the crew and a dinghy which was trailed behind carrying stores and equipment.

On the morning of this expedition an RAF bus from Abyad arrived at our quarter in Kensington Village having picked up a few other people en route. We were taken to a wharf where the launch was able to tie up to take us on board. There were about ten children and eight adults. The journey across took an hour or so.

As we drew near the shore of the Sinai all we could see was a great expanse of silvery white sand for as far as the eye could see, not a tree or a shrub in sight.

The launch anchored a little way from the shore and the children swam the distance between the launch and the shore. The dinghy was rowed in carrying the stores and anybody who did not want to swim the distance.

The very first thing that had to be done was to erect a large awning as respite from the sun.

We had no sooner stepped ashore when we saw in the distance a camel and its rider coming at great speed across the desert heading in our direction.

The camel was travelling at a gallop. I had never seen a camel gallop before, they look quite graceful when they are in action.

The camel and rider were from the Sinai Police Patrol.

The rider looked very smart in his blue uniform and the camel wore a beautiful blue harness; both were very well turned out, and the camel was groomed to perfection. I had never seen a well-groomed camel before. The ones I had seen were mangy and generally dishevelled. The look on the camel's face gave the impression that he knew he was beautiful.

We were questioned as to what we were doing, where we had come from and where we were going. The policeman seemed to be satisfied with our answers, but I dare say a careful watch was kept on us from a distance.

The children found this all very exciting and it would be a lovely story for them to tell their friends when they returned to their schools in the UK.

We all lent a hand with rigging the awning and were very thankful for the shade it gave when we sat on the sand to partake of the wonderful lunch that Leigh had provided.

The children had a lovely time in and out of the water and playing games until it was time for us to start on our return journey.

It had been a most exciting and happy day and we all thanked Leigh for his excellent organisation.

A Commissioner from The Boy Scout Association, which at that time had its Headquarters at 25 Buckingham Palace Road in London, was sent out on a tour of the Middle East and on his itinerary was the Canal Zone. To coincide with his visit a Scout Rally was staged on the Parade Ground at Fayid for all the Scouts and Cubs in the Zone.

The local Scout Commissioner very kindly invited me to attend. At the Rally I met the Commissioner from London. He was very interested in all we were doing and he said that he would like to visit me to have a chat. I invited him to come to our house the next day for lunch.

We had a most interesting meeting and I could see he wanted to help me all he could. He was worried that the Girl Guides could not camp; it was far too dangerous to contemplate them doing so whilst the political situation was so strained and he appreciated that fact.

I explained that we held training days and taught the girls to pitch and strike a tent, they learnt to make gadgets and their knot and rope work was good. I even took him into our garden to show him the flagpole I had had erected in order that the Guides should learn to hoist and lower a flag. He was most impressed and said with a sigh, "What a pity all this training cannot be put into practise." He then added that he thought he knew how we could safely let the Girl Guides camp.

By this time we were both in need of a cup of tea and I went off into the kitchen to make a pot of tea. As we sat drinking our tea I listened to what Ken had to tell me; we were using Christian names by this time.

It appeared that there was a large barrack area on the shore of Lake Timsah next to Moascar, which at present housed The 5th Royal Inniskilling Dragoon Guards who were stationed there. To one side of the barrack buildings was an open space which was used from time to time for activities other than military. The Scouts had often camped there and Ken felt quite sure that when he had spoken to the Commandant in charge of this area, the Commandant would allow the Girl Guides to camp there also.

Security could not be better he assured me as sentries from the Inniskilling Dragoon Guards patrolled the perimeter fences night and day.

I thanked Ken for his interest and concern and promised that I would take along two Guiders and we would meet the Commandant and view the site. If we thought it was safe we could perhaps hold a camp there at the end of December. Ken then went upon his way, leaving me with plenty to think about.

It was not until a few days later, when I met one of the Scout Leaders, that I learned that Ken was Assistant Camp Chief at Gilwell Park - The Associations' International Adult Leader Training Centre - on the borders of Epping Forest and London. In 1952 when he came on his Middle East Tour, Ken was actually Camp Chief's Deputy. No wonder he was so keen that our Girl Guides should camp.

The political situation had improved over the last few weeks since the scare we had just before the children arrived from the UK. No doubt the presence of more troops had made a difference.

One evening there was a knock on our front door and when I opened it there stood our old suffragi, Mustafa. He was all smiles and said that no longer were the suffragis frightened to come to work for the British and he would like to return to work if we would have him.

I had found it a great trial cooking in the excessive heat we were having and I was ready to welcome him with open arms, but I had to show restraint. I told him that if we took him back he was to stay and not go off again as it caused too much trouble. He was full of apologies and promises.

Mustafa started back at work the next week as I needed time to make arrangements for Holdsworth, the batman, to return to his Unit. I was worried that Holdsworth would find it tough back in barracks; he had a gentle nature and I feared he would be bullied. He had been happy living with us and was always willing to help. I would like to have kept him but we could not have a batman and a suffragi. The suffragis did the cooking so it was far more sensible to have the suffragi. I could hardly believe my good fortune when I did not have to go into the kitchen to prepare meals. All I had to do now, was to inspect the kitchen and give Mustafa the menus for the day. This left me more time for other things.

One morning I was paying a visit to the British Military Hospital and I took Ian with me for the ride, Susan had gone to visit one of her school friends. Outside the hospital was a small parade ground and on this ground was a small platoon of soldiers from the island of Mauritius. I was only going to be a few minutes in the hospital so I left Ian stretching his legs around the parade ground.

The Mauritian soldiers had been put 'At Ease' by their Sergeant whilst he went into the hospital. The soldiers were very relaxed laughing and joking amongst themselves. Ian sensed this jolly atmosphere and thought he could join in.

When I emerged from the hospital there was Ian standing in front of the platoon doing the complicated exercise of putting hands on knees and then crossing hands and knees in opposite directions. The soldiers were trying to copy him but they could not do it. They were falling about with laughter when I came on the scene. Fortunately I was able to whisk Ian away before the Sergeant returned. I was laughing myself as it was the funniest scene imaginable.

The weeks had slipped by far too quickly and now it was time for us to go on two weeks' leave to Cyprus. The parents and the school children who had come out from the UK had, at some time, to take a passage on *The Charlton Star* in order to have their children in Cyprus at the appropriate date, to catch the plane back to the UK. Some, like us, were taking two weeks' leave prior to the departure date.

Leigh had found it hard work caring for his three children single-handed and decided that two weeks' leave in Cyprus was a good idea. We all went over on *The Charlton Star* together and then travelled on to the Troodos Mountains where we were to spend our leave period.

We disembarked at Limassol which is the second largest city in Cyprus. The British developed the port and improved the town when they began their rule in 1878. I would have liked to linger awhile in Limassol, to wander through its quaint back streets.

I wished I could have visited the old Castle and St George's Chapel, where Richard the Lionheart, during the time of the Crusades, married in 1191, Berengaria of Navarre and later saw her crowned Queen of England by the Bishops of York and Evreux.

All this, and much more, I would have to see at a later date, for now we were to find a taxi which would take us to the Troodos Mountains, a journey of thirty miles, where we would be based for the next two weeks.

The Troodos Mountains cover most of the central region of the island with peaks rising from 5,000 to 6,000 feet with the highest peak, Mount Olympus, soaring to 6,404 feet. Today in the 1990s the British have installed a radar station on the summit of Mt. Olympus, but no such thing was there in the 1950s.

Cyprus, because of its location in the Eastern Mediterranean, has through the ages, been in constant conflict with surrounding foreign countries. It has been invaded so many times and ruled by many dynasties – Assyrian, Egyptian, Roman, Byzantine, Lusigrian, Ottoman and British, to name but a few.

From 1878-1960 Cyprus was under British Colonial Rule. In 1960 it was granted Independence whilst remaining in the Commonwealth, with the British retaining two military bases and naval bases.

Politically, it remained unstable with the Greeks and Turks forever disagreeing, until in 1974 the Turkish Army invaded the island from the North and overran the northern third of the country.

This led to partition and large numbers of Greeks were expelled from the Turkish Zone crossing over into the Greek Zone. A comparable number of Turks crossed over in the opposite direction. No amount of intervention from other powers, including the United Nations, has been able to alter the situation and Cyprus to this day remains in this unhappy state.

The village of Troodos nestles in the slopes of the hills, which are wooded with pine and cypress trees, with magnificent views over the surrounding mountains.

Above the village of Troodos the British had established a large rest camp for the British Forces stationed in the Middle East. It was an ideal place for relaxation and idleness and could be likened to the hill stations in India.

There was a camp for Officers and their families and a separate camp for Non-Commissioned Officers and their families. These were accommodated in chalet-like rectangular huts made of wood with curved roofs of corrugated iron. There was a front door leading on to a small veranda, a window in each side wall and a primitive latrine and washing facilities attached to the rear of the hut.

The huts were adequately furnished with two beds, two armchairs, a table and somewhere to put one's clothes. Wash rooms were in a separate building, one for the menfolk and one for the ladies. The Officers and NCOs each had a large communal dining room with the catering services run by the NAAFI. Recreation facilities were also available.

The troops' camp was further down the hill in a wooded area. They were under canvas with large square tents with the sides rolled up during the day for coolness. There was always a lovely smell of burning wood coming from the camp as they cooked on open field ranges. They had plenty of space for recreation and there was a relaxed atmosphere about the camp.

For the first two days, Norman, the children and I were content to wander along the mountain paths with the scent from the pines and the magnificent views. The air was cool and invigorating and we were enjoying the sense of space and freedom.

Ian had heard that the waters around the coast were ideal for snorkelling. We had brought our gear with us so there was nothing to stop us from trying it out.

Norman suggested that he would look after Susan in camp whilst Ian and I went to the coast for the day going on the native bus.

We chose Kyrenia, hearing that it had a fascinating harbour and some good beaches.

Ian and I set off the next morning starting very early. Boarding the bus was quite an experience. The village folk were on their way to market with baskets of fruit, vegetables, eggs and even live chickens in crates. The bus was crammed to overflowing. It was a long journey stopping so many times at little hamlets to let the occupants of the bus on or off or just to nip into a cafe for a quick drink, nobody was in a hurry.

It was all most interesting. We found Kyrenia with its picturesque little harbour, horseshoe in shape, with many boats of all shapes and sizes at anchor. The harbour is surrounded by old houses many of them built in the colonial style. There was only one hotel alongside the harbour but many quaint tavernas.

We had to walk a fair distance to find a beach suitable for Ian to attempt to snorkel but were told that Famagusta had the best areas for snorkelling, so we planned there and then to take a trip to Famagusta and hoped Norman and Susan would come with us.

At the end of our return journey, Norman and Susan were waiting for us at the bus stop. We were able to tell them that we had had a lovely day and about our plans to go to Famagusta. We ate a hearty meal in the dining room that evening and retired to bed quite early, for the next day we were to go on an expedition to the summit of Mount Olympus to see the sunrise. We had planned this expedition with Leigh and his three children and another family was joining us.

The summit was only a walk of a few miles and a climb of 450 feet, so we would be able to make it and get there in time.

We reached the summit well before sunrise. As we watched, the sun rose like a ball of fire turning the tops of the mountains into a golden glow. Every nook and cranny was filled with light except for the sides of the hills that were away from the rays. These were deep in shadow, in great contrast. It was a spectacle never to be forgotten.

Two days later all four of us went on the native bus to Famagusta and found it to be a snorkeller's paradise. There was a long sandy beach with just a few houses, small hotels and trees alongside it. At the end of the beach was a lovely bay with rocks and pools. In between the rocks, the pools were deep enough for swimming and this is where Susan and I spent most of our day. Baby octopuses lay resting in between the rocks. Susan was fascinated with them and went off to find a stick so that she could tickle them to wake them and make them move. Norman and Ian had to take it in turns to snorkel. They seemed to spend so much time under water that I was worried most of the time; sometimes they were looking blue when they surfaced. They both said that the marine life under the water was so interesting that they lost all sense of time.

All too soon we had to catch our bus back to Troodos. We had had a most wonderful day.

It was now Wednesday of the second week and Ian was to catch the plane, with all the other children who had been flown out from the UK, on Saturday for their return journey. We noticed that Ian was very quiet and that same evening he was running a temperature. We became very concerned and asked the Medical Officer of the Camp to come to see him. The MO could find no symptoms of a cold or an upset stomach and gave his opinion to the effect that Ian was fretting because he did not want to return to the UK and school.

We felt terrible as it was imperative that he should go back, as much as we would love to keep him with us. He had to be educated and this we could not do in Egypt. The only thing we could say to him was that we had been told, on good authority, that arrangements would be made, early this time, to bring the children out for the Christmas holidays.

I counted the weeks to Christmas and tried hard to cheer up Ian. Susan was almost as bad as she did not want her brother to return either. Oh dear! Life is full of joys and sorrows.

Saturday came and Leigh, ourselves and a few other families were taking taxis to Nicosia to see our children off at the airport. The converted bomber was there to take them back. We hoped that when they next came out they would come on a modern chartered plane and have a more comfortable journey. We all hated the thought of the children having to take that long tiring journey home again.

It was so hard to say goodbye to Ian, we had all been so happy during the summer holidays.

We had little heart to go back into the camp that evening. We wished we could go straight back to Fayid, but we were not due to return until Monday morning.

As I look back to the happy days in the 1950s that we spent in Cyprus I feel so sad for the courageous Cypriot peoples, they have suffered so much strife. It is a lovely island with mountains, forests, flowers, fruits, vines and wonderful beaches. The whole island is steeped in history and religion.

Six

Settling In For The Winter Months

On our return from Cyprus we found it pleasant to be back in Kensington Village again. Mustafa, the suffragi, had made a good job of looking after the home and everywhere looked spic and span. Tiddles our cat was pleased to see us and Mustafa had fed the chickens and eaten the eggs, as I said he could. All was well and home is home wherever it may be.

There was a quantity of mail which had arrived whilst we had been away. All mail had to be addressed to the E.M.E. Directorate so we did not receive it until Norman went into the office, which was the day after our return.

In the mail was a letter for me from the Division Commissioner of Girl Guides, Mrs Anne Thompson. I opened it with apprehension guessing what it might be. Anne had told me a few weeks back that she and her husband were returning to the UK and in this event she wished to appoint me Division Commissioner in her place. This letter was confirming the appointment. Although I felt it an honour to be asked I also felt overwhelmed at the prospect of being in charge of all the Girl Guides, Brownies and Sea Rangers in the whole of the Canal Zone.

I had discussed it all with Norman and he had said that he would support and help me all he could. He had been a great help all along and was most patient when sometimes he would come home to find equipment all over the house and the Guides hastily trying to make a retreat as they saw him coming. Susan was a Brownie so she would feel involved also.

Anne said in her letter that my Warrant had arrived from Imperial Headquarters in London and she wished to present it to me at a meeting of Guiders and Local Association members in Moascar.

The day I went into Moascar to receive my Warrant, I first visited the Area Commandant in the barracks on the shore of Lake Timsah. Ken, the Scout Commissioner from London, had paved the way for my visit.

To reach the area I had to go through the main gates of the barracks. I had no difficulty when the sentries of the 5th Royal Inniskilling Dragoon Guards stopped the official car I was in and made a few routine enquiries. They quickly directed me to the Commandant's office which was attached to his own quarters on the edge of the recreation area.

He knew about me and that I wished to inspect the site with a view to bringing the Girl Guides to camp in the area. He gave me a warm welcome. We discussed many things and I asked a lot of questions whilst drinking the coffee that he had sent for when I arrived.

My main concern was security. He assured me that armed guards patrolled night and day the perimeter fencing which encircled all the barracks and the recreation area which we would use.

He also assured me that if we did set up camp, we would have great respect from the troops in the barracks. They would be warned in advance that we were to have the utmost privacy at all times.

He then took me around the site, explaining that we would have two large square tents for the Guides and two smaller tents, one for myself and one for the two Captains I would take with me. Electric light would be in the tents and the girls would sleep on beds and blankets would be provided.

This did not seem like camping to me, but then we would have more time to pursue camp craft other than pitching tents. Some parts of the area were wooded and this would provide shade and be most pleasant for our activities.

On the whole I was quite impressed and the Commandant had been most helpful. When I left I thanked him and said that after I had discussed things with my Guiders I would let him know our decision.

Fortunately I was able to discuss all this with Anne before the afternoon meeting. She was all for it and wished she was going to be around to visit us, but alas she and the Brigadier were leaving in two weeks time.

With my Warrant in my hand I set off back to Fayid wondering how I would feel when Anne had left and I was responsible for both the North and the South Districts.

Most people, during the hot weather months, had had a happy time. The beach had been well and truly used in our efforts to keep cool. Now in the cooler months we would be settling in and keeping ourselves occupied in various ways. Living as we were, under restrictions and virtually isolated made us fall back on our own resources. All kind of activities would be starting and soon the place would be one social whirl.

Norman and I joined the Scottish dancing club. We had always enjoyed Scottish dancing and the young man who ran the classes was a Scot with a broad Scottish accent. He enjoyed teaching and we enjoyed learning.

Susan was excited as her school was putting on a play. This play was centred around two main characters, a Mr & Mrs Snook. Susan was to be Mrs Snook. We would hear her going around the house practising her lines and I was to make her a dress with a long skirt.

The drama and operatic societies were busy practising for the shows they would put on in a few weeks' time. With the drama there was much talent around and last Christmas they had put on a pantomime which was much enjoyed by everybody. The operatic society was brave also and attempted a Gilbert and Sullivan production.

A little way across the sand from our quarter was a hard tennis court. This was much in demand and I soon found that if

Landing on the Sinai Desert showing the awning erected as respite from the sun

The Sinai Desert Police Camel Patrol

CANAL ZONE NEWS

PRINTED & PUBLISHED UNDER THE AUTHORITY OF THE COMMANDERS-IN-CHIEF MIDDLE EAST

Peter's sermon. "God hath made the same Jesus whom ye crucified, both Lord and Christ."

No. 44 Tuesday, February 12th, 1952

WAR MINISTER'S TELEGRAM TO THE QUEEN

The following is the text of a telegram sent to Her Majesty the Queen by the Secretary of State:

"Mr. Anthony Head, with his humble duty, begs leave to offer on behalf of the Army Council and the Army an expression of their profound sympathy with your Majesty and the members of the Royal Family. We had followed with anxiety the course of the severe illness of His late Majesty but the news of his sudden passing came as a great shock. The Army will ever remember with gratitude the keen and practical interest which His late Majesty always showed in its progress.

In reply, Her Majesty sent the following message:

"I greatly appreciate the kind message which you have sent to me on behalf of the Army Council and the Army. Please convey to all ranks the sincere thanks of myself and my family for their sympathy. ELIZABETH R."

OUR LAST ISSUE

MESSAGE FROM GENERAL SIR BRIAN H. ROBERTSON, BT, GCB, GBE, KCMG, KCVO, DSO, MC, ADC

During the three months of its life, the Canal Zone News has performed a valuable service. It is now being discontinued in its present form because the supply of newspapers has become easier. Those who have been responsible for its production deserve our thanks for a good job well done.

Extract from 'Canal Zone News', dated February 12th, 1952

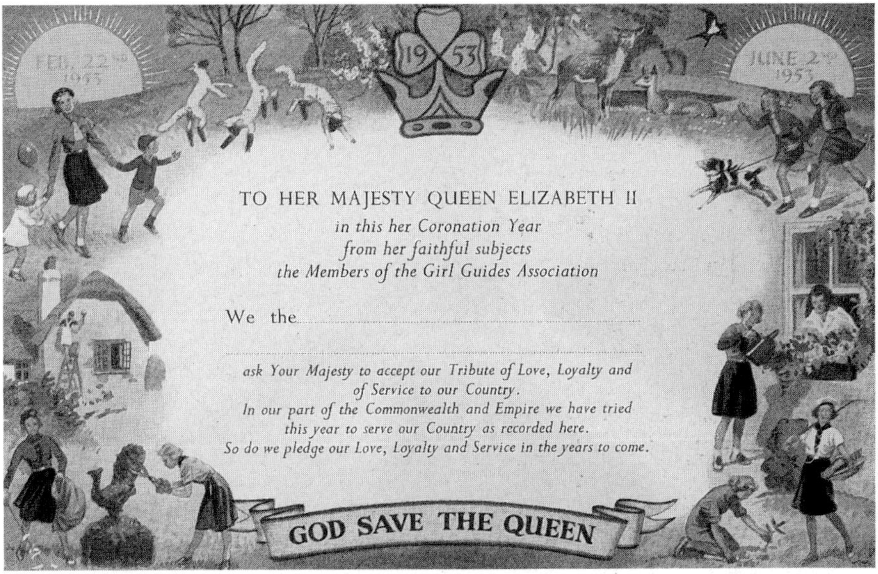

The Coronation challenge sent to every Girl Guide unit in the Empire and Commonwealth

ISSUED FREE

Issued by F.B.S. Canal Zone
Vol. 6. No. 12. (New Series)
1420 Kilocycles 211 Metres

FORCES' RADIO TIMES

Programmes from September 6th to 12th 1953

F.B.S. COMPETITION

Valuable Prizes for the best three entries
Closing Date: Saturday 26th September, 1953
Read the Rules Carefully

RULES.

Below there are nine programmes taken from our current programme schedule. Write down which is your favourite "programme" out of the nine programmes listed below and give in thirty-five words, or less, the reason why you like it the best.

EXAMPLE:— World Theatre. Because FBS are presenting some of the world's finest plays with the world's finest casts and I always stay in Tuesday Nights especially to listen.

The Decision of the judges will be final.

No members or relations of FBS Staff may enter for this competition.

Highways and Byways	Sunday	11.00-11.30
Dan Dare	Monday-Friday	17.45-1800
FBS Jazz Club	Monday	21.00-21.30
The Record Changer	Monday	21.45-22.30
World Theatre	Tuesday	20.30-22.00
The Curtain Rises	Thursday	21.00-21.30
The Friday Concert	Friday	21.00-22.00
Star Billing	Saturday	20.45-21.00
Mood for Dancing	Saturday	2130-2230

Address your entries to:— FBS Competition
No 3 Forces Broadcasting Station,
GHQ MELF 17

And make sure that you post your entries to reach this station not later than Saturday 26th September 1953.

The results of this competition will be printed in the Radio Times and announced over the air in The Canal Zone News.

Thought for the week

"This above all: to thine own self be true,
And it must follow, as the night the day,
Thou canst not then be false to any man.
Act 1.Sc 3. Hamlet (Shakespeare)

The Week's Sport

ASSOCIATION FOOTBALL

A commentary on the second half of one of the day's League matches can be heard on Saturday at 1645 hrs.

Front page of 'Forces' Radio Times', dated September 6th to 12th, 1952

1745	DAN DARE. Pilot of the Future
1800*	THE NEWS AND NEWS TALK. Followed by the Weather Forecast
1815	THE CANAL ZONE NEWS
1830	AG's HALF HOUR. Illustrated talk by Mrs McCallum on the Guide Rally in Cyprus, July 14
1900	LETTERS FROM HOME. Presented by Pauline Cowie
2000*	THE NEWS AND HOME NEWS from Britain

Extract from 'Forces' Radio Times' showing author's talk

Inspecting the Sea Rangers

Some of the patrol leaders, who went to the camp on the shore of Lake Timsah, in their summer uniform

1st Kabrit Brownie Pack

Mohammed joining in the fun

Ian with his gadgets in the garden

Susan's birthday party on the beach

Ian enjoying the winter sunshine on his last trip out

I wanted to play it was a question of booking the court well in advance and finding one's partners afterwards.

Norman and I took up fishing again and would go out to Fanara Wharf at weekends. Susan came with us but this year she did not have our neighbour's children to play with, as our new neighbours were not interested in fishing. Susan would quickly become bored and we would have to pack up early. We did not mind as we usually caught two or three large lute in a very short time and this was plenty for our pot and we could share the catch with our friends. Mustafa was well used to cooking the fish the way we liked it. It was this time last year, before the suffragis left, because they were too frightened to work for the British, that Mustafa first started to cook the fish we caught. It certainly gave variety to our meals.

Writing mail home took up a great deal of our time. We wrote to Ian a lot and our parents once a week. We were receiving happier letters from Ian now that he had been out for the summer holidays. He was much more contented and realised that all he had to do was to travel in an aeroplane instead of a train or car to reach home at the end of term. Every week when we wrote we ticked off on the calendar one more week to the Christmas holidays and the weeks went by very rapidly. We already had received notification that we should send in application forms to request that our children be put on the list if we wanted them to be flown out for the Christmas holidays. This time they were to fly by chartered plane from London to Port Said, all very simple after the tortuous journey of last time.

There was also one's own entertaining to do with cocktail and dinner parties to be arranged and so it would go on, with never a dull moment.

Families were beginning to trickle back from the UK now that the political situation was much improved. Those families who had been sent back to the UK this time last year could now return, providing their husbands had accumulated sufficient points on the points system, to allow them to return. Gibraltar

Village was filling up again. This meant that the Guide Companies and Brownie Packs would increase in numbers and some girls would pick up where they had left off.

There was great excitement in the Guiding world, as the Captain of the 1st Fayid Company was to be married. Her fiancé was a Civil Servant and working for S.I.M.E., Special Intelligence Middle East. He was based at GHQ and resided in the Officers' Mess. Ruth was a physiotherapist working at the British Military Hospital and living in the nurses' quarters in Fayid. Norman and I were guests at the wedding and the Girl Guides formed a guard of honour as Ruth and her husband came out of church.

It was a strange coincidence how Ruth became Captain of the 1st Fayid Company. She had gone on leave and was staying in the United Services Club in Ismailia. Here, one morning she was taking a walk around the Club garden, which overlooked Lake Timsah, when she met another person doing the same thing. They began a conversation and soon found that they were both interested in the Girl Guide Movement. The other person was none other than Anne the Division Commissioner. It was not long before Anne was telling Ruth to contact me when she returned to Fayid.

I was delighted when Ruth came to see me as the present Captain of the 1st Fayid Company was leaving. Her husband's term of duty was at its end and they were returning to the UK. The Company was thriving and I needed a good Guider to take over. Ruth was a happy individual and just the right person to take over the Company.

At my last Guiders' meeting and also at a Local Association meeting there had been lengthy discussions on the subject of the Guides camping at the Lake Timsah site. Finally, for the first run we thought it best that I and two Guide Captains should take sixteen Patrol Leaders. In this way all the Companies would be represented and the knowledge the Leaders gained could be passed on to the other Guides in their Companies.

Fortunately I had two Guiders with camping experience but no one with a Camper's Licence. A date was fixed and we were to spend four nights in camp. There was great excitement as camping had not happened before in the Canal Zone. I felt that Ken, the Scout Commissioner from Gilwell Park, who had given me much encouragement, would be pleased that we had taken the plunge.

I shall never forget the morning when two Army trucks, with an armed guard on each, rode out through the checkpoint at the entrance to Kensington Village. The trucks were filled with sixteen Guides, the two Guide Captains and myself plus kit bags, stores and equipment. Happiness abounded as we waved farewell to the crowd of well-wishers who had assembled to see us off.

We arrived at the site early in the afternoon. There was much to be done if we wished to have the camp running smoothly before nightfall. The store tent was pitched and gadgets made to form shelves on which to place our stores. A flagpole was made and erected, tripods made to hold the hand basins which went inside the wash tents when they were put up. A stand was erected for the washing up next to a table where the food would be prepared. Latrines were already on site, so we were saved from that hard work.

The sixteen Guides formed four patrols with four Guides in each, each Guide taking it in turn to be Patrol Leader for the day. This arrangement worked very well.

We were all feeling tired by the time we had finished these things and so we went early to bed in readiness for a busy and happy day on the morrow.

I was up early in the morning to have the 'Orders of the Day' pinned to the notice board before the rising whistle was blown, so that each Patrol would know their duties for the day.

With only four patrols all duties were spread between them. Wood and Water Patrol, whose duty it was to collect and stack the wood for the kitchen fire and to keep the boiler going for hot water for washing and washing up. Vegetable Patrol, whose duty it was to prepare all salads and fruit and to peel the potatoes. Mess Patrol, who served all meals, after which each girl would wash her own utensils. Camp Patrol, who were responsible for the tidiness and cleanliness of the camp and to provide the Colour Party for the day. The two Captains and I supervised the cooking.

We had declared, before we left Fayid, that Sunday should be an Open Day for parents and friends to visit the camp. This would give the Guides lessons in hospitality as we said that tea would be provided for the visitors.

I looked around the camp and was well pleased with what I saw. Every girl was busy doing some kind of work or project, and I hoped when our visitors arrived the next day they would see a smoothly running camp with a happy atmosphere, just as it was on this day.

We had noticed a latchgate which led out on to the beach beside the Lake - a wonderful place for a camp fire, we thought.

The Commandant had expressed a wish to visit us in camp and we had invited him to come at 4 o'clock when we would be brewing mugs of tea. We mentioned the latchgate and asked him if we would be allowed to go through the gate and hold a camp fire on the beach. To our great joy he said "yes". He also said that whilst we were there he would alert the guards as to our whereabouts.

It was fortunate that we had the wooded area as the Wood Patrol was able to collect sufficient wood for our camp fire. After supper, just as it was getting dark, we went through the gate and selected a good place. The fire was soon burning and we settled down to an evening of yarning and singing. There were some very good singing voices among the Guides and the sound as it wafted across the Lake was really beautiful.

The part of the beach we were on was just alongside the Ship Canal. The cutting was on a higher level and we could just see the tops of the ships as they glided through. The crew of one ship as it slid past in the darkness saw our fire and heard us singing. They trained their searchlight on us and gave us a friendly "whoop! whoop! whoop!" on their siren. This was a magical moment.

It had been a happy day and the evening had been special. We made sure that the fire was well and truly out before we left it, with no traces of it ever having been there. Before we left the beach we sang 'Taps', the Girl Guide song for the ending of a day. 'Taps' was introduced to the Movement at the First International Conference at Oxford in 1920, by the USA delegates. It was adopted as the Girl Guide/Girl Scout closing hymn. The tune adapted to that of the 'Last Post'.

The word 'taps' was originally applied to the tapping on a drum which in the American Army was the signal to retire. When later, the bugle was introduced the call retained its original name.

'Taps' could never have been more stirring and beautiful than it was this evening. The sweet voices of the Guides as they sang the poignant words and the haunting melody, rang out over the still lake and lingered on and on over the water.

'Taps'

Day is done,

Gone the sun,

From the sea,

From the hills,

From the sky,

All is well

Safely rest

God is nigh.

We all slept soundly that night, too soundly for our own good it seemed!

At about 5.45 a.m. I was awakened by three Guides standing by my bed. One of them was saying "Commissioner, Commissioner, please wake up." I roused myself and was quite cross at being awakened so early. I sat up in bed and said, "What are you girls doing up at this time in the morning, go back to bed and wait for the rising whistle." There was almost a wail from Betty, the Guide who had spoken, as she said, "But Commissioner I woke because I was cold and I went to put on my sweater which I had put beside my bed before I went to sleep and it was not there." The story continued. Betty had then awakened her friend in the next bed and told her. They both searched for Betty's sweater but in the process of doing so found that her friend's clothes were missing also. They then became worried and came to tell me.

At first I thought it was a prank until one of them said, "But Commissioner, where are your clothes?" At this I got up and put on the electric light in my tent. Lo and behold the clothes which I had placed on a chair beside my bed were no longer there. I had also placed on a small table, just beside where my head lay on the pillow, a thermos flask of cold water, a torch, a clock and my sponge bag; all were missing.

I went into the two tents where all the Guides were awake by this time. They had all gone to bed with two blankets on their beds, but now most of them had only one and from each bedside clothes were missing. It was all most puzzling. We must fetch the Commandant I told them. I left the two Captains with the Guides in the large tents to reassure them that no harm would become them.

The three Guides who woke me and I set off across the open ground to fetch the Commandant. What a scene it was! I was wearing a pair of white pyjamas with navy blue polka dots all over them, over these I wore a camp skirt which I found in the corner of my tent. The Guides put on what ever clothing they could find or borrow from somebody else.

We looked a right motley crew as we knocked on the Commandant's door. He came to the door in a pair of yellow and red striped pyjamas with a dressing gown over them. His face was a picture of incredulity as we told him our story of having been robbed.

We all traipsed back again to the camp looking even more of a motley crew, with the Commandant in front, I behind and the three Guides following on.

The Commandant gave one look in the tents and said he would send for the Military Police. I asked for time to allow the Guides to get up and dress themselves in whatever they could find in the way of clothing. By the time this was done the atmosphere in the tents had lost its tension and in its place was much laughter as each one looked at the other in borrowed clothes which were either too large or too small.

Whilst we waited for the Military Police to investigate we went to prepare and have breakfast. It appeared from the Police findings that just to one side of the area where our camp was, there was a small inlet of water from the Lake. This had a pipe going across it and it was here where signs were shown of feet going backwards and forwards over the pipe. There must have been quite a number of Egyptians to have achieved removing the amount of blankets and clothing from the tents and to have passed them back over the pipe.

I had heard stories of how Egyptians could remove bedclothes from soldiers whilst they were asleep, even managing to remove a sheet or blanket from underneath a soldier without waking him. This was done by tickling the soldier's back very lightly with a feather. This did not wake him but caused him to roll over until with adept hands and much patience the sheet or blanket could be removed. I had never really believed this story, but now I could well imagine it to be true.

As soon as we could we held a meeting to sum up the situation. The part that worried us the most was that in the afternoon our visitors would be arriving for our Open Day.

I put it to the Guides that anyone who felt they would like to go home with their parents or friends when they arrived, would be free to do so.

I had spoken with the Commanding Officer of the 5th Royal Inniskilling Dragoon Guards, I could not help thinking that somebody would get into trouble when such a thing could have happened under their very noses.

Sincere apologies and sympathies were expressed and the CO said that he hoped we would stay for the next two nights and assured me that extra security would be put on.

I had left the Guides to talk amongst themselves and now went back to hear what they wished to do.

Not one of them wanted to go home and their answer to me was, "Girl Guides do not quit." I felt so proud of them. "Right," I said. "Let's buckle to and smarten ourselves first."

There was a great swapping and borrowing of clothes from one another and much laughter in the process, until in the end the result was quite reasonable. Our visitors arrived, Norman and Susan amongst them. Norman was shocked when I told him that we had been robbed and said, "Of course you will pack up and come home." I gave him the answer I had received from the Guides. He was quite surprised but gave a smile of satisfaction. All our visitors saw when they arrived was a tidy and happy camp with no traces of there having been trouble. Fresh blankets had been brought in from the Quarter Master's Stores and now each Guide had two blankets nicely folded back on her bed.

That night and the one after, when we slept, the lights were left on and we knew that the night patrols would be very much on the alert, so nobody was worried.

Two days later the Army trucks came to take us back to Fayid. The camp had been a success and all the Guides were in high spirits.

The Local Association was wonderful. They held social events to make money in order that the Guides who had lost clothes and property could be reimbursed.

The weeks were flying past and now Christmas was looming. Ian, with the other school children, would be arriving in two weeks.

We had heard that some of the returning families would also be on the chartered plane, filling up the empty seats. One of the REME Officers was expecting his wife. How lucky the families were to travel by plane instead of having to take the long sea voyage on a troopship.

This time an Army coach would be bringing the children and extra families from the aerodrome at Port Said to a meeting place in Fayid.

We were so excited on the day of their arrival and went early to meet the coach. As the coach swung into the meeting place there was the happy smiling face of Ian half out of the window.

It used to be intriguing to watch the young Officers meeting their wives. For months we would have entertained them and come to know them. When their wives arrived their personalities seemed to change and they appeared to be quite different. One had formed an image of what the wife would be like. It was quite a shock as the pre-conceived idea was completely shattered when she arrived.

Fayid was buzzing with activity. Restrictions around the local area had been lifted and this meant we could visit Ismailia, but for lengthy journeys armed escort still had to be applied for.

The weather at this time of year is always very good; bright sunshine with just a little nip in the air night and morning. Ian was enjoying the sunshine and thought how lucky he was to have a few weeks respite from the English winter. Everybody was busy making plans for the Christmas festivities. The NAAFI was working overtime to supply all the stores we would need. I never ceased to marvel how efficient the organisation was. There was a great number of mouths to feed and it was surprising how little luxuries would turn up from time to time.

The womenfolk were greatly relieved that this Christmas the suffragis were back, as it would be they who would be cooking the Christmas dinners and dealing with the temperamental oil stoves and primus stove, I had toyed with the idea of making the Christmas puddings myself, but then decided against it. Mustafa said he could manage and it really was best to stay out of the kitchen.

The Garrison Church was beautifully decorated with flowers sent in from people's gardens. We had a new Padre, he had only been with us for a few weeks and was fulfilling his pastoral duties very well, relating sympathetically to the families and the Troops.

On Christmas Day we had invited four unattached Officers and it was so lovely to have Ian with us this Christmas.

Mustafa with a smiling face and well satisfied with himself presented an excellent dinner.

I think attending the Christmas Service in the Church in the morning and the feeling of goodwill when greeting one's friends sets the feeling for the rest of the day.

This was our second Christmas in the Canal Zone and it certainly was a happy one.

Seven

Coronation Year Of Queen Elizabeth II

Tel-el-Kabir was a large Military Station, isolated in the desert on the road to Cairo. It was the last outpost of the British Forces in the Canal Zone.

To reach it from Fayid one took the road to Ismailia, turned west on to the road to Cairo, passing a military vehicle depot, then on into the desert passing the large Royal Air Force station of Abu Sueir. After Abu Sueir there was nothing but desert until reaching Tel-el-Kabir. Restrictions on this road were never lifted and vehicles were required to travel in convoy. Two cars could travel in convoy but had to have an armed guard in each car.

It was New Year's Eve when Norman and I, together with Ian and Susan, travelled to 'TEK', an abbreviation for Tel-el-Kabir. Norman was on official duty so we could travel in a Military car with driver and armed guard. We needed to tie up with another car so that we could travel together.

We were to stay as guests of a REME Brigadier and his family. The Brigadier was Norman's opposite number in Tek and had been stationed there for two years. I had met him and his wife back in England and I was looking forward to meeting them again. They were enthusiastic Scottish dancers and had invited us to attend the Hogmanay Ball put on by the Scottish Dancing Club of Tel-el-Kabir. We learned of another family also going to the Ball from Fayid so here was our second car for the journey.

It was a bright sunny morning when the two cars set off. We were all ready to enjoy the journey, the children full of excitement.

The journey was going well until we had gone a few miles past Abu Sueir, when one of the cars developed engine trouble. The car teetered on for a bit until it finally stopped. We were completely isolated and had no means of communication. Whilst the two guards covered us with their rifles the men folk attempted to start the car. It just would not budge. There was only one thing to be done and that was to cram everybody into the one car and continue our journey.

It was the most awful squeeze. The two drivers and the two guards wedged themselves into the front of the car, whilst the four adults and the four children crammed themselves into the back.

Although we were apprehensive we nevertheless saw the funny side of the situation and it was amusing when we reached the gates of Tel-el-Kabir to see the look of astonishment on the face of the soldiers as we extricated ourselves one by one from the car. A vehicle was quickly sent from the workshops to retrieve the broken down car.

We enjoyed our stay in TEK. It was a friendly station and the social side of life was very much alive.

The Hogmanay Ball was celebrated in true Scottish style. The ballroom looked very colourful with many kilts worn. Norman was only sorry he had left his kilt in England, but then we really had not envisaged his needing it in the desert.

This visit to Tel-el-Kabir had been most opportune for me as it enabled me to visit the Girl Guides and the Brownies. There was one Guide Company and one Brownie Pack. Although they were not holding meetings over the New Year, when they heard I was coming they arranged a special meeting in the school hall. The Chairman of the Local Association also got her Committee together to meet me. It was encouraging to see that they were working well with enthusiastic Guiders.

The four days went all too quickly and soon we found ourselves waiting at the check point to join up with other cars to make a convoy for our return journey to Fayid. After Ismailia we did not need another car to resume our journey.

The next week we were to say farewell to Ian when he left with the other school children to return to the UK after the Christmas holidays. When next they came it would be for the summer holidays. It always took all our strength to say goodbye to Ian when we put him on the coach which would take the children to the airport. We all hated it.

We were now going into 1953 which was the year of the Coronation of Queen Elizabeth II. Her Coronation was to be in June and we in the Canal Zone would be well to the forefront with our celebrations. Already plans were being made for big events and everything would have the prefix of 'Coronation'.

Soon it would be time for the Khamsin, a hot SE wind which blows so hard it causes sandstorms which can last for three or four days, and come and go for fifty. No big event would be put on until the Khamsin was out of the way but it was a good time to make plans.

Early in February I received a large parcel from the Girl Guide Headquarters in London. It contained a large quantity of decorative envelopes which formed the basis of a Coronation Tribute. It was a scheme devised in England and Girl Guides in all parts of the world would be participating.

Inside each envelope was a record card. Each Company, Pack or Crew were challenged to find ways to help others and to spread goodwill. They had three months to work on this challenge and when finished they would write on the card what they had done. It was to be a collective effort, no individual names were mentioned. Record cards were selected and sent to London and if chosen there, would be sent to the Queen as a token of loyalty and love from the Girl Guide Association.

This tribute and challenge kept everybody very busy for the whole three months. Many enterprising tributes were thought up. The Sea Rangers made a layette for the first baby to be born in the Canal Zone nearest to the day of the Queen's Coronation.

For many days in the beginning of May, Aircraft Carriers, Cruisers and Destroyers came sailing through the Great Bitter Lake and on into the Canal. They were ships of the Royal Navies of Australia and New Zealand and from the Navies of India and Pakistan. Their mission was to join with ships from other nations of the world, for the Review of the Fleet at Spithead in Portsmouth, to mark the Coronation of the Queen.

The Aircraft Carrier *HMAS Sydney* from Australia was the first one to be seen sailing into the area of the Lake. It was a magnificent sight silhouetted on a calm lake. Every day for a week we were out with our binoculars looking at the ships as they passed by. They were an inspiration to us all and spurred us on with our own plans to celebrate the Coronation.

The first major event was a Coronation Ball put on by RAF Abyad. A large marquee was erected on the Parade Ground, floodlit, which looked impressive as one went through the main gates. The lighting inside the marquee was artistically placed so as to enhance the spectacle of the brightly coloured uniforms worn by the Officers.

The RAF Officers wore their tropical white monkey jackets, a short closely fitting jacket, with the Royal Air Force blue tightly fitting trousers. The Naval Officers also wore their white jackets but they had plenty of gold braid on theirs and their trousers were navy blue, also with tight legs. The Military Officers wore an array of colours, some with scarlet jackets with navy lapels, others with navy jackets and red lapels according to their regiment or corp. Some regiments even wore mustard-coloured jackets with contrasting lapels. Their trousers are usually tight-legged with coloured braid down the side of each leg.

It was amazing how well turned out the ladies were, considering that there were no dress shops in Fayid, and Ismailia could offer very little. I expect there were many hours spent at the sewing machines, which is what I had done. There was one hairdresser in Fayid but he was not much good and certainly could not rise to hairstyling.

The chefs in the Abyad catering had excelled themselves and even produced a boar's head as a centre piece on the large buffet table. One could only praise RAF Abyad for arranging such a magnificent evening to start off the Coronation Celebrations.

Moascar was holding a Coronation Sports Day, with teams from all the Services competing. Things like this had to be staged before the weather became too hot. I remember the Sports Day in Moascar very well. There was a great number of spectators. Areas were roped off for the segregation of the ranks. In the first enclosure were the high ranking Officers, such as Admirals, Rear Admirals, Generals, Lt. Generals, Major Generals, Air Marshals and Air Vice Marshals accompanied by their wives and families. The next enclosure was for Naval Commanders, Brigadiers, Colonels, Lt. Colonels, RAF Group Captains and Wing Commanders and their wives and families. The segregation went on right down to Non-Commissioned Officers.

I got into serious trouble from Norman. The wife of one of the Air Vice Marshals who was President of the Canal North Local Association of the Girl Guides, saw me and as she wanted to discuss an important matter with me, she beckoned me over into her enclosure. Norman was out of our area at the time when I stepped over the dividing rope and went to speak with the Air Vice Marshal's wife. When Norman came back he spotted where I was and when I returned he said in a very worried voice, "You know you are not supposed to be in that enclosure. What on earth do you think you are doing?" I hastened to tell him that when I had been beckoned, it would have been very churlish of me not to go.

It is easy to realise that the senior wives get lonely in their positions and being able to mix with other wives and make friendships through doing something like the Local Association work alleviates their loneliness and does not cause them to lose rank. I had learned this fact very early on when I had formed the Local Association.

The Sports Day was an interesting event with the Navy, Military and Air Force competing against one another. It was rather like a Tattoo.

The Sea Rangers, Guides and Brownies were busy planning their Coronation events. The Brownies held their Coronation Revels in early May. Numbers in the Packs had increased with the return of the families from the UK and an influx of new families to fill Gibraltar Village.

Canal North District was able, this year, to travel to Fayid by using the Army school buses. These always carried armed guards and the political situation was thought to be stable enough to allow the girls to travel on these buses.

This meant that on the day of the Revels, May 16th, Brownies from Tel-el-Kabir, Abu Sueir, Ismailia and Moascar would come to Fayid to join with Packs from Shallufa, Kasfaret, Kabrit, Fanara, Abyad and Fayid.

The number of Brownies combined with Guiders, helpers and parents would be several hundreds.

The Old Victoria Football Enclosure was booked and the Military Band of the Inniskilling Dragoon Guards was to play for the afternoon, by kind permission of their Colonel. The amount of help we received from the Army, the Local Association and the parents was amazing. The afternoon was a delight. Brownies are so rewarding to work with, they give you their all.

The Girl Guides and Rangers Coronation Swimming Gala was also a day of coping with large numbers as once again Canal North District travelled to Fayid.

The Army Physical Training Corps were magnificent. Weeks before the event the instructors would come to the swimming pool to instruct the girls. The standard of swimming, diving and life saving was very high and the spectators enjoyed the day equally as much as the Guides and Rangers themselves.

I had received notification that the General, as Commander in Chief, would like the Sea Rangers and the Girl Guides to join in the Grand March Past of the Forces. This was to be held at the close of a Drumhead Service on Coronation Day itself, which was June 2nd, 1953. This was indeed a great honour and much practising went on to perfect the girls' marching abilities.

I was becoming increasingly worried at the amount of official transport I was having to request to enable me to organise and coordinate all the events that were in progress. With this worry on my mind, I went to see the Colonel in charge of Transport.

He quickly put my mind at rest by saying that the Commanders of all the stations were very aware of the hard work put in by the Guiders and that Guiding and Scouting was helping to ensure that the children of the families in their care were kept occupied and happy whilst having to live the isolated life imposed upon them.

As to my requests for transport to take me to the stations and to attend meetings, the way had been made clear. They had given me the title of 'Families Welfare Adviser' and as such I would go down in the books authenticated by this title.

I felt as I left that I ought to be wearing "another hat", but it was satisfying to know that the work was recognised.

On June 2nd, which was the day of the Coronation of Queen Elizabeth II, a Drumhead Service and Grand March Past was held on the Parade Ground in Fayid. A vast number of people were assembled and all waiting for the ceremony of the hoisting of the Union Flag. The Royal Navy was given the honour of supplying the Colour Party. The Colour Party stepped forward and proceeded to attach the flag to the halyards by way of the toggle and to pull the flag up. It reached the top but somehow got twisted and would not unfold. The young Naval Officer pulled on the halyard when the flag squeezed itself in between the toggle and the halyards. The Lieutenant went on pulling and finally when the flag emerged and flew, it was upside down. Everybody felt terrible that on this day of all days such a thing should have happened.

There was nothing that could be done about it apart from feeling desperately sorry for the Naval Lieutenant who I feel sure would never live the incident down.

After this everything went extremely well. The Service was conducted by two Military Chaplains, one from Moascar and our Chaplain in Fayid. Rousing hymns were sung and everybody joined in wholeheartedly.

The Grand March Past left nothing to be desired. It had been well-rehearsed and when the Scouts, Sea Rangers and Guides brought up the rear it made us feel as if we were one large happy family celebrating.

In the 1950s loyalty to one's Queen and country was very strong; nobody questioned it. Now in the 1990s patriotism is not so popular and the younger generation are seeing the popularity of the Monarchy on the wane. Anti-establishment seems to be the order of the day. It is sad, because to 'belong' is so important.

With all the events and celebrations finished there seemed to be an anti-climax but it did not last long.

RAF Abyad had started an Open Air Cinema. They ran films which had been imported from the UK. It was very pleasant to sit in the open air on a warm evening watching the films, sitting on comfortable arm chairs. These were placed in the first half a dozen rows and were reserved for Officers and their families.

It made a pleasant evening out and was welcome at this time of year. It was popular with the troops and airmen and Abyad ran a show every fortnight during the hot weather months.

A few weeks back the Girl Guide Association of Cyprus had written to me telling me that they were setting up an

International Camp in the Troodos Mountains in the second half of July and they would welcome British Guides in Egypt. I had written and reserved fifty places for the Guides from the Canal Zone.

I would now have to turn my thoughts to the organisation of this adventure. When I had notified the two Districts of this Camp there had been a good response and the fifty places were soon taken up.

I did not know how the Guides and Rangers would travel to Cyprus, so I went to see the Army Authorities to talk over this problem. The Colonel in Transport thought it best for all concerned to use aeroplanes from RAF Fayid. Being told this, I went next to see the Commanding Officer of RAF Fayid, who was, as usual, very helpful.

The girls were to attend the Camp in two contingents of twenty-five Guides each, staying for one week, changing over on the next week. The CO said that two planes would be necessary and when the change over was due, the planes taking the second contingent could bring the first one back.

I had expressed a wish to the Army Colonel of Transport that I might be allowed to pay a visit to the camp but I could not be away from home longer than a weekend.

He said he would give me permission on one condition and that was that I would agree to give a talk on the Forces Broadcasting Service on my return, telling everybody about the Camp, this I was very willing to do.

RAF Fayid booked the planes and I quickly wrote off to the Girl Guide Association of Cyprus to arrange for the planes to be met at Nicosia by the camp bus which would take the Guides up to the Camp in Troodos.

Each Guide was to have two blankets in her kit for use in the cool nights in the mountains. These were going to make their kit bags heavy and more weight for the small planes the RAF used, for ferrying purposes, to carry.

The Major-General of the Royal Army Ordnance Corps lived in a quarter opposite ours in Red Flannel Alley in

Kensington Village. I went to see him to ask if it would be at all possible to ship fifty blankets over to Cyprus in one of the corvettes that plied backwards and forwards from Cyprus to Fayid carrying stores and sometimes passengers. He said this would be a simple operation and he would be pleased to set it in motion when I gave him the dates. His daughter was one of the Sea Rangers attending the Camp.

The blankets arrived safely at Limassol Port and were picked up by an Army truck. Unfortunately the soldiers on the truck misread the instructions and took the blankets to a WRAC Camp somewhere on the Island.

This was terrible as the Guides did not have blankets for the first night. The camp staff managed to keep them warm somehow and the next morning a great search was mounted to find the blankets, They were located and post-haste sent up to the camp. The Major-General was none too pleased when he heard of the mix up.

There were Turkish, Greek, Armenian, American and British Guides in Camp. It was a wonderful experience for the fifty Guides who attended the Camp. I often wonder if they knew just how lucky they were to have this experience, also it is not very often Girl Guides go to camp in aeroplanes.

I found the Armenian Guides most interesting, many I spoke to would not see their parents for another four years. They came to school in Cyprus for six years and did not return home during that time. How important Guiding must have been for those Guides especially during the long summer vacation. The feeling of friendship and sisterhood must surely have helped to lessen the hardship of being away from home for so long.

I was very pleased I had travelled over for the weekend. It enabled me to thank the Island Commissioner for inviting us from Egypt and I was able to thank also the Commissioner for Training who had worked so hard in our interests and had taught our Guides so much.

During the weekend I was able to make notes for the broadcast I was to give on the Forces Radio Station when I returned to Fayid. I knew also that some of the parents would be calling or phoning to my house to hear first-hand accounts of how their daughters were enjoying themselves.

Now that the Coronation events and festivities were over, I was looking forward to a well-earned rest and a few weeks of relaxation with my family.

Eight
The Last Summer Of The Tour

It is now 1953 and this summer would be the last when Ian would be flying out to join us. He would come once more after that, for the Christmas holidays. Norman's tour of duty would end in May 1954 after which time we would be returning to the UK.

We had decided not to take leave in Cyprus but to enjoy life on the beach here in Fayid with our boat and beach hut. Ian and Susan enjoyed going out in the boat so much that it seemed a pity not to make full use of the facilities we had.

Although the days would be hot, Norman finished work at lunchtime and we could then go off to the beach in the early afternoon. We could always rely on a breeze coming up directly the sun went down. The drop in temperature caused thermals which sent ripples across the lake and as soon as we saw this happening we knew that the breeze would follow. This was our relief from the heat of the day.

The school children from the UK arrived at the end of July. It was a joy to meet them; they brought a breath of fresh air to the place. Ian complained that it had seemed a long time since the Christmas holidays and he said that it was so good to be back.

Susan had her eighth birthday during the holidays and to celebrate she had a party on the beach for ten of her friends. The beach was an ideal place to hold a children's party. The beach hut and awning provided sufficient shade for all to sit under and there we had the birthday tea. We thought it too risky to take other people's children out in the boat, so they swam, played games and ate ice cream sundaes from the clubhouse.

Just a few days after Ian arrived Mustafa, the suffragi, came to me and said that he was forced to go home to his village because of a family crisis and he would have to leave at once. This was a nuisance as for a few days until we could find a replacement, I would have to do the cooking. I did not relish the idea of cooking in the heat and coping with the temperamental oil stove and primus once again.

Norman went in search of a suffragi. It was no easy task and five days went by before we could find a replacement.

Norman brought along a boy from Ethiopia for me to interview. He seemed to be about thirty years of age and looked strong and healthy. He had had experience in cooking and had worked for the British before. We said we would give him a month's trial.

I was thankful to have the help. Ian and Susan had been very good and had helped with the sweeping; what a lot of sweeping one had to do. Living in the desert meant that the sand blew into everything.

Kassay was the name of the new boy. He did not wear a galabiya, a long loose robe, like the Egyptian servants and Arab men wore, but was rather smart in his dress. In the evenings when he waited at table he wore black trousers, a white shirt and black bow tie.

If he had any spare time he spent it digging in the garden. I found that he was collecting beer bottles in the kitchen and putting them in a large cardboard box. One day when we had been out all day, we returned to find that he had placed these beer bottles upside down and at an angle all round the edges of the flower beds, to make as he said "a neat edging to the beds". I did not like the look of it at all but when I saw Kassay waiting at the gate to show us what he had done and the huge smile of satisfaction on his face, I had not the heart to tell him I did not like it.

When he had time off he would dress himself up wearing a suit and a trilby hat and go off into Fayid. He would always comeback crestfallen as the Egyptians would be unkind to him and ridicule him.

One day when he had been out he was so angry on his return that he stormed into the garden saying, "When I get back to my country I will turn their water off, they have my water and I will stop it, then they will all die." It appeared that the fresh water we were using was piped all the way from Ethiopia.

Poor Kassay he was not happy away from his country. He stayed only a few weeks and then went back to Addis Ababa.

Mohammed came next and he was a conventional suffragi. He was fond of children and when Ian and Susan were in the garden with Ian erecting what he called his 'gadgets', which were pulleys and ropes fixed to trees in order to give Susan rides in a bucket, Mohammed would go out and sit under the trees to watch them, fascinated as Ian pulled on the ropes to carry Susan at a height from tree to tree. Ian and Susan spent many happy hours like this and it was at these times that Norman and I were pleased we had not gone on leave to the Military Camp in Cyprus. The only real walk we could take that was outside the Fayid area but in close proximity to it, was to climb the largest of the few hills that lay behind Fayid. These hills always looked so inviting with their mauve and pink colours as the sun rose and again at sunset.

The largest of these hills was called 'The Flea' and was approximately 1,500 feet high and could be easily walked if one started early in the cool of the morning and descended as the sun was going down in the afternoon.

We fixed a day to do the walk and asked Leigh to join us, his children had not come out this summer as his tour of duty was to end around Christmas time. Jill, her husband and their two children made up the party.

We set off early in the morning to do most of the walk before the heat of the day. It was not a hard climb but was rocky and very barren, the only living things on the hill were ants and lizards.

We reached the summit just before noon and stood gazing down at what we saw below. Fayid and the Lake lay beneath us, the Lake still and shimmering in the noonday sun. We could see Kensington Village, Gibraltar Village, the NAAFI and its warehouses.

To the right was the British Military Hospital and the Nurses' Quarters, further on, the new Canal Road which ran alongside the Lake and was built by the British so that the Military vehicles could travel backwards and forwards without the hazards of going through native villages en route. We could make out Fanara RAF Station and Fanara Wharf, where we did our fishing.

On our left was GHQ with the numerous wooden huts that housed the various Army Units. It was amazing what we could pick out: the Officers' Club on the shore of the Lake, the Clubhouse of the Non-Commissioned Officers and the Troops' beach. The Church in Kensington Village looked most impressive with the quarters clustered around it. Further to our left was RAF Abyad and RAF Fayid.

We could only marvel to see this great organisation which ticked over day by day supplying the needs of the Troops and the families that were there. Its only purpose to keep the peace whilst ensuring a safe passage through the Canal for the ships on their shortened route to India and the Far East.

The top of 'The Flea' was rocky with deep crags and crannies. These gave shelter from the hot sun and the gusts of wind which tore up the side of the hill.

Norman was sitting in one of these crannies pouring himself a drink from a thermos flask when a great gust of wind came sweeping up the cranny. It took the thermos flask right out of his hand and sent the drink all over him. He was not at all pleased, as not only was he wet all over, but because we had lost a third of our drink.

The children had enjoyed the adventure and had amused themselves by throwing stones down the crags and crannies to see how long it took before the stones came to a stop.

We arrived down in Fayid in time to have a quick bathe in the Lake before dusk which was most refreshing after our climb.

A Royal Navy Cruiser had been anchored in the Great Bitter Lake for a few days. We all wondered why it had been there so long. Through GHQ a message was sent round to say that the ship would invite fifty children from Fayid and the surrounding areas to a tea party to be held aboard ship. This was particularly popular with the boys but a few girls went as well.

The children assembled at the jetty and boats came out from the ship to fetch them. They all had a wonderful time and came back not wanting much supper after the scrumptious tea they had been given. The boys were inspired by their tour aboard the cruiser and many said, when we met them, that when they were grown-up they would be sailors on a big ship like that.

It really was a kind gesture on the part of the Navy, but I expect it gave the crew something to do whilst being anchored for days with no chance of a trip ashore. Security could not have coped with sailors coming ashore even if there had been anywhere for them to go or anything for them to do, but there was nothing in Fayid to attract sailors, as well the Navy would have known.

A week or so later GHQ planned a boat trip around the Lake ending up at a lagoon further along the Lake nearer Suez. Although this trip was a pleasant day out it was not nearly as exciting as the one Leigh had planned last year when we landed in the Sinai Desert.

The days flew past with many things to do. Ian and I played tennis a lot and Susan was busy with the friends she had made from the resident children.

At almost the end of the summer holidays and before the school children flew back to the UK, Norman planned a day trip to a place called Ein Suckna which is on the shores of the Red Sea. Twelve of us went in two Army trucks with a driver and armed guard in each truck. The journey took us right along the Great Bitter Lake, using the Canal Road, until we got to the edge of the Red Sea. The Red Sea curves into two or three bays before one reaches Suez about thirty miles further on. The first bay is Ein Suckna and this is where we stopped.

It is a picturesque place with hot springs and a few low hills close to the shore. As we approached the bay the colours of the sea, the sand and the hills took our breath away. The sea was very blue and the sand a soft golden yellow whilst the hills were all colours going from dark mauve to pink tinged with blue. Truly an ideal place to spend a day relaxing and keeping cool by bathing in the water.

The Red Sea is very salty and therefore very buoyant. When swimming it is very difficult to keep one's rear under the water. This fascinated Susan and we have a lovely picture of her swimming with her bottom out of the water. We found some lovely shells on the beach and one enormous conch shell which we still have today.

Norman and Ian used the snorkelling gear but did not find much in the way of fish or coral to look at.

We had to start our return journey early in order to be off the road before dusk. The four soldiers had taken it in turns to swim whilst keeping a watchful eye for any intruders.

At the time set for our return we all assembled at the trucks which we had left parked on the sand. To our horror we found that the trucks had sunk into the sand up to the middle of their wheel hubs. Nobody had thought of this possibility.

Everybody turned to and helped to dig the trucks out. Ian found some wood on the beach and brought that along to put under the wheels. When we finally got the trucks moving it was a question of jumping on the trucks as they went along for once started they could not stop.

We had two older people with us and they were allowed to get in the trucks before they started. The men folk almost threw the children in, whilst the rest or us had to be very agile.

We reached home safely without any more mishaps and all felt that it had been a most pleasant day.

The summer months slipped by happily and now it was time to get back to a daily routine. Once more we had said farewell to the school children and seen them on the way to catch the plane that would take them back to the UK, where they would be met by grandparents, aunts or uncles or guardians before they returned to their various schools.

This time I had longed to go back with Ian as last term he had left his Prep School and this term he was to start at his Public School, Framlingham in Suffolk.

All summer we had been in contact with both schools to ensure the change over would go as smoothly as possible for Ian. It must have been horrible for him not to have his parents there to see him safely settled in.

In normal times I would have returned to the UK and would have been there when he changed schools, but with the situation as it was in the Canal Zone, had I gone I would not have been allowed back into the Country and this would have caused worse problems. It is at these times that Service life becomes hard.

The change over had put a great deal of strain on the Grandparents who were acting as Ian's guardians. The two Grandmothers were to share the tasks of buying and marking the uniform and preparing from a long list, things needed for a boarder, and to pack his trunk.

I remember so well the letters that went from us to them and from them to us to try to smooth out the conflict of ideas as to how the things should be done. The Grandmothers were both strong characters and both of them wanted to do their best.

I received a letter from my mother complaining bitterly that she had packed Ian's trunk and when she saw it the next day, it had been completely repacked by the other Grandmother who thought she could do the job better. Somehow Ian arrived at the school with everything he should have had.

I found it difficult to settle for a few days but there were many things awaiting my attention and I needed to start on them at once.

The Girl Guide units had started their weekly meetings and I took a check to see how everything was going.

Both in the North and South Districts there had been a few changes. The constant flow of Army personnel coming and going as tours came to an end and fresh people were posted out, made it inevitable that numbers in the Companies and Packs would go up and down.

If daughters of the new families joined the Brownies or Girl Guides as soon as they arrived in the Zone then in three years they had learnt a lot. This was particularly noticeable in the Guide Companies where many of the girls gained their First Class Badge. It was always exciting for me to go to a Company to present a 1st Class Badge as this meant the girl had worked very hard to achieve it.

We did not keep them long enough for them to become Queen's Guides, but with the training they had received from us they would be well on the way and could continue when they returned to the United Kingdom and gain their Queen's Guide Award there.

It was difficult when Leaders had to be changed, this would mean more visiting to the units to instate new Leaders and again to present Warrants when they arrived from the County Commissioner in Alexandria or Imperial Headquarters in London which ever the case may be.

The RAF Station of Abu Sueir had had a change of Commanding Officer and his wife had accompanied him. I heard that the wife was young and was worried about the Girl Guides and Brownies in her Station and unsure about taking over the duties of Chairman of the Local Association from her predecessor.

I arranged a day when I could go to Abu Sueir to meet her. I would be away one night as I needed to visit Tel-el-Kabir to give the Guides and Brownies there encouragement.

On the appointed day a large limousine arrived at our quarter with the GHQ pennant flying from its bonnet. It was early in the morning and Norman had not yet left for work. His car came to take him to work but it was not nearly as large as the one I had been allocated. He smiled as he waved me off and said, "It is surprising what a turned-up hat can do!"

I was wearing my best uniform with the silver flash of a Division Commissioner on the side of my turned up hat with the badge of British Guides in Egypt at the base of the flash. In later years Headquarters in London changed the velour hat which was turned-up on one side to a large beret type hat; in my mind not nearly so smart.

I arrived in Abu Sueir at about noon after waiting in Moascar for another car to travel in convoy down the road which led to Cairo.

I went straight to the quarter of the Commanding Officer. His wife came out to greet me but I could sense she was nervous. I noticed as we sat talking that she was looking at me with a puzzled expression. After a while she burst out laughing and said, "Thank goodness you are normal," and quickly added that she had worried all night because the Girl Guide Commissioner was coming.

It appeared that that morning she had gone to her wardrobe and chosen the most sombre clothes she could find and had taken her make up off feeling sure that I would be stuffy and drab in my dress. She continued to laugh and said, "I need not have worried because here you are smartly dressed, wearing lipstick and are quite normal."

I suggested that she go and change and put her make-up on again. After this the atmosphere was really good and when her husband, the Group Captain, came in for lunch he was quite amused by the story.

Once installed as Chairman of the Local Association, she worked very hard for the units in her Station.

Early evening I went on to Tel-el-Kabir and spent that night with Norman's opposite number in the REME. We had not met since the whole family came last New Year's Eve for the Hogmanay Ball.

The Guides and Brownies were doing well and in spite of being so isolated there in the desert, surrounded by barbed wire and sentries on the perimeter, their spirits were high and they were eager to hear all about the other Companies and Packs in the South District and said how much they had enjoyed coming to Fayid for the Coronation events.

My return journey to Fayid was a most pleasant one. At this time of the year, when the heat of the summer had passed, one could really enjoy the desert. I loved the soft pale greens of the foliage with the contrasting deeper green of the date palms, the yellowness of the sand accentuated the little oases I passed on the way. The Sweet Water Canal flowed quietly alongside the road and belied its deep secret of being the most polluted water imaginable.

On the other side of the road the fellahin were working their meagre crops or attending their sheep or goats. The few camels I saw made it picturesque whilst the fellucas moved with such grace over the Lake that they seemed to present a timelessness all of their own.

As the car sped on its way I pondered on the unnatural situation that existed here around The Canal and thought what a pity it was that guns, barbed wire and soldiers were everywhere.

Norman and Susan were very relieved when my car drew up at our quarter and deposited me safely home again.

There was always anxiety if anyone was travelling on the roads.

Nine

Winding Down

It is a strange thing that when you are on a three year tour of service the thoughts of returning home do not hit you until about six months before the termination date.

Whoever devised three years as an operative span of time for a tour must have been very clever, because the first year you are settling in, the second year doing all the things there are to do, whilst the third year becomes a repetition of the second and if you are not very careful can become monotonous.

It had only just dawned on me that in a few weeks there would only be six months left of our tour. The thing uppermost in my mind was that I must start looking for a replacement of my appointment as Division Commissioner of the Girl Guides in the Zone.

This was not going to be easy and I would need all the assistance I could muster. Meetings of both the Local Associations were due and this is where I would broach the subject.

The first meeting for the North District was held in Moascar at Flagstaff House and the Division Secretary and I set off from Fayid to attend it.

A representative from every Station was present and the General's wife presided over the meeting. When I announced that I would be returning to England in six months time and that we must start looking for somebody to take over my appointment as Division Commissioner there was dead silence whilst the news penetrated. Then everybody said they would do their best and ask around their Stations and when newcomers arrived they would see if amongst them there was anybody with Guiding experience. The meeting continued with the rest of the agenda and at the end of the proceedings there was plenty of lively chat over a cup of tea.

Before starting the journey back to Fayid, I visited the bathroom which was on the first floor of Flagstaff House. I was just preparing to descend the staircase when I caught the eye of the Division Secretary who smiled up at me from the hall below. She looked very pleased that the meeting had gone so well so I gave her a nod of satisfaction and in doing so missed the top step and went hurtling down the staircase from top to bottom.

The Division Secretary and I sat on the fourth or fifth stair from the bottom, I nursing a bruised and bleeding leg.

The General who had a young wife, having married for the second time, had a small son who was cared for by his English Nanny. The Nanny who was taking a tray of tea up to the Nursery on the first floor, passed us on the stairs. She looked down at us as she passed and said in great surprise, "We often have the children sitting on the stairs but never the grown-ups." Soon after this the General came out of his study and came to the stairs and looking down at me he said, "Oh you poor lady! Is there anything I can do?" I thanked him profusely and said I was fine.

I was thankful that I had not to drive myself home. I needed a few days to rest the leg before it was better. To this day I can still feel how foolish I felt sitting on the stairs at Flagstaff House.

When Canal South District Local Association held their meeting they greeted my news with great concern and they also promised to begin a search for a willing person to take over from me.

In the next few weeks I sounded out the Guiders. All of them were frightened by the thought of the work involved and the travelling the job entailed. There was also the element of the constant change in service personnel. WRENs and Nursing Sisters were amongst the Guiders.

It had been fortunate that I had been approached within two weeks of my arrival in the Canal Zone. This meant that I had had a long stretch of just over two and a half years, I arriving five months later than Norman.

Although I was constantly thinking of this problem, I was determined to shelve it until after Christmas.

The build up to Christmas was now in full swing with the school plays, the drama shows and the round of parties.

The Scottish Dancing Club had started its classes again and was working up to the Hogmanay Ball which was going to be held in Fayid this year with the Clubs of Ismailia and Tel-el-Kabir coming to us. Norman and I went every week to learn the dances so that we could really enjoy the Ball.

Ian arrived for the Christmas holidays and we were very anxious to hear how he had settled in at Framlingham. He looked very grown-up and smart in his Harris Tweed suit which was the uniform of the school. It appeared that Ian liked his house master who had been very kind to him when he arrived at the school. He mentioned two boys by name with whom he had become friendly. The parents of one of the boys had invited him out to lunch with them when they were visiting their son one Sunday. This was very good news and cheered us immensely.

We now began to plan our own Christmas, invitations had gone out to young Officers who were either unmarried or waiting for their family to join them, the point system still being enforced. This year we had also sent out invitations to two Nursing Sisters from the British Military Hospital, which they gladly accepted.

I discussed with Mohammed, the cook/suffragi, the menu for the Christmas Day dinner. We would have the meal around midday as travelling after dark would be too risky for our guests. I asked Mohammed if he could cook a traditional Christmas pudding and he said he could. It was amazing how the suffragis could cook all the English dishes. They would have gained experience as they went from household to household, each lady of the house teaching them to make their own favourite dishes. If a suffragi did not know how to cook a special dish then he would ask a suffragi from another household to come to show him how to do it. They would never lose face.

Mohammed cooked an excellent meal and brought along a young boy from his family to help him. He made a delicious ice cream to go with the Christmas pudding. I was puzzled as to how he could have made such a nice ice cream. There was no fresh milk or cream to be had in the Zone; we had to rely entirely on tinned evaporated milk for everything.

Later I asked Mohammed how he had made the ice cream. He smiled, but did not keep the secret to himself, willingly he gave me the recipe. It was none other than a tin of evaporated milk! He said the milk must be chilled first and all the utensils chilled before whisking the milk for a long time whilst adding three tablespoons of icing sugar and a little vanilla essence. When the consistency was correct it was put into the freezing compartment of the fridge until it was needed.

I still have the recipe written in my recipe book under the heading 'Mohammed's Ice Cream'.

Christmas Day had been a great success. Asking the two Nursing Sisters had been a good idea and made for a lively gathering around the table.

On Boxing Day we dined with friends who had two children the same ages as our two. Ian on the last two journeys out from the UK had met their son on the plane. They seemed to have a lot to talk about and Susan and their daughter were in the same class at school, so everyone was happy.

Ian was very conscious that this was the last time he would be flying out to us and said that he was going to make the most of it, particularly the lovely sunny weather. We had almost forgotten the dark dank days of winter in England and we were reminded of them more than once by Ian who kept expressing his joy of the bright sunny days of December and January in Egypt.

I had been invited to a Coffee Morning by the wives of RAF Fayid. It was a small station but a very friendly one and always seemed to be busy. The aircraft based at the airfield were in constant use for local flights and ferrying duties to and from Cyprus.

I was talking to a group of wives, one of which was the wife of the Commanding Officer. I was telling them that we were nearing the end of our Tour and I wished I could buy some suitable material to make my daughter an overcoat. Susan had completely grown out of the coat in which she had travelled to Egypt. When we disembarked in early May she would need a coat.

The CO's wife said, "Why don't you apply for an Indulgence Flight in one of the planes that go two or three times a week to Cyprus?" This was news to me. I had not heard of any Indulgence Passages being allowed.

The wives said they often popped over to Nicosia to do some shopping and if I went I could buy the cloth for Susan's coat.

What a wonderful idea! I was so excited when I came home and told Norman all about it. He had not heard that Indulgence Flights were being granted.

All I had to do was to apply for the flight and then turn up in time to catch the plane. The planes left early in the morning and stayed in Nicosia long enough for the wives to do their shopping in the morning and then to have lunch before catching the plane back.

I did not want to miss this opportunity and booked for a flight early the next week. Norman took me by car to catch the plane and met me from the return flight. Oh what a lovely shopping spree I had!

I found just the correct weight of material for Susan's coat and found buttons and lining in the same shop. I also was able to buy presents for the folks at home.

Ian had returned to the UK. It had not been so painful seeing him off this time as we were able to count the weeks until we ourselves would be home.

Out came the sewing machine and I went to work on making Susan's overcoat. I would be able to wear the coat I had brought out with me. It did not look too out of fashion.

We wives always hoped we were keeping up with the fashion but it was difficult. We relied on magazines and gleaned what we could from the latest wives out – that is if they themselves were fashionable.

I was becoming increasingly worried about the Girl Guides. There were 350 Guides, Sea Rangers and Brownies in the Canal Zone and they had to be kept together.

I had worked incessantly in my efforts to find somebody to take over from me and the Local Association had been diligent in their search.

I held emergency meetings of the Guiders in both North and South Districts. Last year I had appointed a District Captain in the South District to help me with the administration and it had worked well. I now appointed a District Captain in the North District.

I wrote to the County Commissioner in Alexandria and explained the situation. In her reply she suggested that I should also appoint a District Secretary as well as a District Captain in each District. The two of them could work together in consultation with the Local Association. She also said that she would answer any queries and would endeavour to visit the Districts as much as the political situation would allow. The Diplomatic Bag could always be used for correspondence, which would speed things up a little.

I compiled a letter to every Guider and Local Association Member telling them how things would be left and in order to make it clear to my readers I am printing the letter. I wrote: -

March 1954

Girl Guides
Canal Zone

Dear

I am relinquishing my appointment as Division Commissioner on March 31st, preparatory to my return to England.

Despite strenuous efforts on my part over the past two months, I have been unable to find anyone to take over from me.

I have therefore decided, in order that Guiding in the Canal Zone shall continue as before, that the Zone shall remain in its two Districts and that each should be controlled independently by a District Secretary and a District Captain. This decision has been approved by Imperial HQ and the County Commissioner.

The District Secretaries will receive correspondence and instructions from Imperial Headquarters London and the County Commissioner in Alexandria.

The District Captain will coordinate all the practical aspects of Guiding, will carry out requirements received from Imperial Headquarters or the County Commissioner, transmitted to her by the District Secretary, and will report back to the District Secretary all matters concerning Guiding in the District.

Neither the District Secretary or the District Captain are empowered on their own to recommend Guiders for the issue of their Warrants. This may, however, be done in consultation with the Local Association, and it is only in this way that Leaders of Guide Companies and Brownie Packs can be appointed.

It will greatly assist if Guiders, before they are due to return to England, will look around for a suitable person to take over their Company or Pack, and to get them to work with them a few weeks prior to their leaving.

They should then recommend these people to the Local Association, the District Secretary and District Captain, for their approval in the appointment.

I thank you for the great work you have put into Guiding and for the support you have given me.

I wish the Companies and Packs great success.

Yours sincerely

Marjorie McCallum

Now we were to turn our thoughts to packing. I hoped every day that Norman would start to pack the things such as our china, glass, cutlery, books, gramophone records etc.. He seemed disinclined to begin this task until one day he came in with four tea chests, opened all the cupboard doors and set about packing.

I can see him now, everything came out of the cupboards. Every room had two cupboards which were deep and went from floor to ceiling. They held a lot and I had to watch that he did not pack anything we would want before we left.

Heavy baggage was always collected two weeks prior to embarkation. All trunks and boxes had to be well-sealed and well-marked.

We had had notice that we were to embark on the Troopship *HMS Empire Ken* on May 4th, 1954. I had all our clothes to worry about and to pack. Susan wanted her favourite belongings to travel with her, which took up one whole suitcase.

In the midst of all this packing I had taken Susan to the British Military Hospital to see the dentist. He said her teeth needed adjustment and he would like to do it before we embarked. The Nursing Sisters said they were short of patients in the hospital and it looked bad if there were no patients on the ward. They asked me if they could look after Susan and keep her in hospital overnight when the dentist had finished the work he had to do. They promised me that they would look after her well, so I agreed. She thoroughly enjoyed herself with plenty of attention and lots of ice cream.

This was the day when Norman came home and found me in tears. He said, "Whatever is the matter?" I wailed at him, "Everything is falling down around me – my daughter is in hospital, my neighbour has just been to take my chickens away and this morning I took Tiddles [our cat] to be put to sleep." He nestled me in his arms and said, "Well old girl, we are leaving one life but we will soon make another." I felt better after that and was able to tackle again the tasks awaiting me.

The worst part of having an animal in these foreign countries is that you cannot leave them as very soon they would be neglected and go like all the other animals one sees – starving and wild. When an animal has been loved, like we had loved Tiddles, it would be cruel to leave them to such a fate.

The Quarter Master came with the Inventory to check that everything that had been issued to us when we went into the quarter was still there and in good order.

There was a bit of a hitch as during our time I had gone down to the Quarter Masters Stores and changed the dining table and chairs; I had not liked the ones I had been issued with and went to the Store to see if I could change them.

I found a very nice oblong table, quite large in a black wood with six chairs to match, it had a sideboard to go with it. I asked if I could make a swap and it was agreed. I was the envy of all families who came to dinner as it really did look good.

The swap had not been noted on the inventory and it took some explaining as to how I had come by the black table and chairs.

I pointed out that I had polished and cherished this table and chairs and that he, the Quarter Master, was getting back much better furniture than I had been issued with. My answer seemed to placate him and all was well. Everything else in the quarter was marked off as being correct.

When we got to the kitchen it was a different story. Mohammed looked very cross as the Quarter Master opened the drawers and cupboards to inspect the contents. Quite a lot of the utensils were either broken or missing.

Poor Mohammed he thought he was going to get into trouble, but I explained that during our time in the quarter we had had Mustafa, two batmen, the Ethiopian boy, Kassay, before Mohammed came. Each one had done their fair share of breaking things.

The Quarter Master does make allowances for a certain amount of wear and tear and breakages but if it is excessive then one would be expected to pay. I think in our case it was thought to be reasonable.

The next thing to go was the car as we had decided to have it shipped back to England.

Our friends and neighbours were popping in all the time to wish us well and a safe journey. We were invited to many a farewell drink around Kensington Village.

On the last evening before our departure Norman and I sat down quietly reminiscing on the happenings of the last three years. We came to the conclusion that our sojourn in Egypt had been a happy one, it had certainly been packed with events. We had made a lot of friends many of whom we would meet again during our service life.

It was a bright sunny morning when the Army vehicle drew up to take us to Port Said. Susan was excited about going on a big ship.

I felt very sad as I looked back at our quarter. It had been very basic but it had been home. I just had to hang on the words Norman had said to me when he had found me crying – "Well old girl, we are leaving one life but we will soon make another." Which is exactly what we did.

Epilogue

The voyage home on the Troopship *Empire Ken* was both relaxing and enjoyable.

On disembarkation we learned that Norman's new appointment was to the REME Inspectorate based at Chislehurst in Kent.

We found a delightful country house in Sevenoaks right opposite a school for Susan. The house had a lovely garden full of rhododendrons and large lawns.

We had been to see Ian in Framlingham and found him happy and well.

Egypt seemed a long way away until one morning when Norman and I were having breakfast and opening our morning mail. There was a letter for me from Imperial Headquarters of the Girl Guide Association. This letter was a great surprise for both of us, it contained the news that I had been awarded the Medal of Merit of the Girl Guide Association for the work I had done for the Movement in the Canal Zone. I had worked hard and it was most gratifying to hear that it had all been appreciated.

We soon made a new life for ourselves. Susan was happy at school and Ian was able to come home not only for the long school holidays but at half-term as well.

The Kent countryside seemed pleasantly green and beautiful after having lived so long with nothing but sand around us.